Praise for *Cutting Myself in Half*

"Way to go, Taylor! I am honored beyond words at being given a place in your transformation. I know what dedication and hard work it took for you to stick to your guns and accomplish your weight loss goal. Great job!"

—**John Schneider, actor**
(aka Bo Duke, *The Dukes of Hazzard*)

"Taylor's approach to better health through physical activity and managing weight has successfully adapted a number of research-based behavioral methods into a teen-friendly format. I believe that its focus on practical self-management will be effective for many over the long term."

—**James J. Annesi, Ph.D., Director of Wellness**
Advancement, YMCA of Metropolitan Atlanta

"Taylor is the embodiment of what the Marines are all about. Dedicated, hard-charging, and mentally/physically alert. The Marine Corps would be proud to have him in the ranks."

—**Lt. Col. Bill Howey USMC (Ret)**

"We applaud Taylor's personal efforts and his willingness to help other teens get healthy. If more teens took personal responsibility for their health and fitness before they enter the workforce, our nation's employers would spend significantly less on healthcare and productivity losses due to unhealthy employees."

—**Beth Reynolds, Wellness Program Manager,**
Alere Medical, Inc.

P9-BZT-724

"Child and teen obesity have reached epidemic proportions in the United States, and it's rare to see someone as young as Taylor take the initiative to confront the problem. Often teens who attempt to lose weight try extreme methods that produce only short-term results. Taylor, however, developed a safe, healthy plan that can keep him fit for life."

—Bob Bagheri, M.D.
(Taylor's doctor since he was three years old)

Cutting Myself in Half

150 Pounds Lost
One Byte at a Time

Taylor LeBaron
and Jack & Mary Branson

Health Communications, Inc.
Deerfield Beach, Florida

www.hcibooks.com

DISCLAIMER: The information contained in this book is not intended as a substitute for the advice and/or medical care of a physician. It is recommended that you consult with your physician before embarking on any eating, exercise, or lifestyle regimen.

Library of Congress Cataloging-in-Publication Data

LeBaron, Taylor.
    Cutting myself in half : 150 pounds lost, one byte at a time / Taylor LeBaron and Jack and Mary Branson.
        p. cm.
    Includes index.
    ISBN-13: 978-0-7573-1359-2
    ISBN-10: 0-7573-1359-0
        1. LeBaron, Taylor—Health.   2. Overweight teenagers—United States—Biography.   3. Obesity in adolescence.   4. Physical fitness for youth.
    5. Weight loss.   I. Branson, Jack.   II. Branson, Mary. III. Title.
    RJ399.C6L335 2010
    616.3'9800835—dc22

                                                                2009040715

Publisher: Health Communications, Inc.
            3201 S.W. 15th Street
            Deerfield Beach, FL 33442–8190

Cover design by Larissa Hise Henoch
Interior design by Lawna Patterson Oldfield
Interior formatting by Dawn Von Strolley Grove

To my mother, Penny LeBaron

I could not have gotten fit without her help.
Sometimes she was sick. Other times, she was tired.
But she always drove me to my workouts.
And her help with my fitness program is small
compared to her support in every area of my life.
She encourages me when I fail and applauds me
on my accomplishments.
I love you, Mommy.

Give Yourself Permission to Be Fit

START FEELING GOOD ABOUT YOURSELF TODAY. Then lose the weight tomorrow. An awesome person is already there inside you. *You know him.* He's funny, he's smart, and he's amazing! You just need to give that incredible person the body he deserves.

Contents

Foreword

If you're a teen who struggles with weight, get ready to change your future. But be warned—the change is totally up to you. You cannot win the ULTIMATE FITNESS GAME unless you take personal control of your eating and exercise. Regardless of the circumstances that brought you to the point of obesity, it's up to you to turn things around.

Blaming people and circumstances is reasonable and fair, but it won't make you a single pound lighter. It's true that schools require you to sit during most of your waking hours, then serve you fattening lunches. It's a fact that restaurants and food manufacturers disguise unhealthy foods in delicious and tempting super-size packages. Everywhere you turn, someone is pressuring you to have another bite, try a new dessert, or clean your plate. While adults may tell you that you need to lose weight, few are setting an example of how to do it.

You can find plenty of people and circumstances to blame, but that won't solve your problem. That won't get rid of the teasing. It won't bring back lost opportunities. It won't help you live life to the fullest. It won't erase the dangers of diabetes, heart disease, or other obesity-related illnesses that may lie ahead if you become an obese adult. Blaming others doesn't get you one step closer to a fit and healthy body.

Parents, doctors, teachers, and friends can be great allies, but you can't rely on them to solve your weight problem. And isn't it true that they don't really seem to understand, anyway? Unless you've been an overweight teen in the twenty-first century, you can't fully understand.

Taylor LeBaron understands. He is one of the fortunate few teens who has found a way to radically transform his body, and he's translated his methods into a system that you can use, too. It's a system presented as a game—a game called the ULTIMATE FITNESS GAME (UFG)—that *you* can learn, practice, and master. Once mastered, you will have taken control of your health, your weight, and so much more.

The skills you use to transform your body are the same skills that allow you to unleash the greatness within you. Learning and applying Taylor's fitness plan will endow you with the confidence and lifestyle that will bring new meaning to "live life to the fullest" and "be all that you can be."

Today's teens are tomorrow's leaders. The future depends on you. The world, as well as your body, is what you make of it. You can take control or just let it slide. You can lead or follow the pack. You can win or you can lose. If you're ready to win, and win big, then read on to see how it's done!

I wish you great health and happiness in the future.

—Michael Dansinger, M.D.
Nutrition Doctor, NBC's *The Biggest Loser*
Nutrition and Weight Loss Expert, WebMD
Diabetes Reversal Program, Tufts Medical Center

Acknowledgments

Have you seen some of the crazy diets out there? One says to eat all protein and no carbs. Another promises that eating only grapefruit and bacon . . . or cabbage soup . . . or drinking apple cider vinegar with each meal will cause a big weight loss. Diets like that don't work for long because one or two foods can't give us everything we need to be healthy.

When I started putting together my total fitness plan, I soon realized that I needed a variety of vitamins, minerals, and other nutrients. Each type of food provided something, whether big or small, that I needed for my body to be strong.

I also discovered that I needed the help and encouragement of a lot of *people* to carry out my fitness plan and to share my story with others. Some played a small but important role. Others played a huge role. But I couldn't have done it alone, and I'm grateful to the following people for their help:

My mother, Penny LeBaron. If the people in my life were parts of a healthy diet, my mom would be the protein. She keeps me strong and gives me constant encouragement. She taught me that anything is possible.

My grandfather, Jack Branson. He's truly one of a kind—a unique and honorable guy. I would do anything he asked of me, without question. He's taught me precision and dedication. He helped me conquer a mountain. He's the calcium that's given me a strong structure.

My grandmother, Mary Branson (Nana). She makes it possible for me to keep my weight off and stay motivated by always complimenting my new look and by providing healthy foods. She has always loved me, no matter what my size. She is truly the best grandmother anyone could ever have. She's the "good carbs," my comfort food.

My brother, Elliott. For a kid brother, he's great. He's told me many times that he's proud of me for getting fit. Elliott's the fiber that I might not always notice, but I'd miss it if it weren't there.

My great-grandmother, Catherine Kinney. Everyone calls her MomMom, whether she's related to them or not. MomMom is one of those people who is proud of her family no matter what. She loves to brag about all of us. She was proud of me when I was more than 100 pounds overweight, and she was proud of me when I lost the weight. MomMom's the natural sweeteners—apples, oranges, grapes—that are always a treat.

Then there are all the vitamins and minerals. They may be measured in teaspoons or capsules instead of cups, but their contributions are powerful:

My uncle Dave (Adam) Branson. He adds the spice to family gatherings. He's worked hard to promote this book, and he takes time to compliment my weight loss.

Marvin and Loretta Harris. Aunt Loretta is an exercise enthusiast, and she's always encouraged me and given me exercise tips. More important, she and Uncle Marvin have encouraged all my endeavors, from bluegrass music to computer programming. And they thought I was cool even when my weight was the highest.

Richard Becker, director of Chrysalis Experiential Academy. He cares about his kids like they were family. He's been as proud of my weight loss and my book as anyone. I'm fortunate to have Richard as my friend and leader. He's turned learning and life into an adventure.

Dr. Michael Dansinger. He has a genuine concern for helping kids avoid diabetes and other weight-related health issues. I'm glad people like Dr. Dansinger work toward a better future for overweight teens, and I'm honored to be working with him to spread the word that fitness is within everyone's reach.

Dr. James Annesi, wellness director for the YMCA of Metropolitan Atlanta. Dr. Annesi develops programs that help adults and kids manage their weight and get fit, and maintain their fitness over time. His program, the Coach Approach, was the backbone of my exercise plan.

Dyan Auterson. Dyan first met me when I was a self-conscious, overweight fourteen-year-old who had more interest in Chips Ahoy chewy cookies than exercise. She challenged me, encouraged me, and instructed me. She was my YMCA trainer, and I'll always be grateful to her. She still checks up on me, and she'll always be an inspiration.

Melba Black, wellness director, Forsyth County Family YMCA. When I'd lost more than 100 pounds, Melba displayed my poster-sized before-and-after photos at the Y. She, along with the rest of the YMCA staff, showed me in dozens of ways that they were proud of me. I'm glad to have this opportunity to thank them.

Katherine Wunder. Katherine has been my friend since I was ten years old, regardless of my size. She never judged me, and she has always made me feel confident and accomplished.

Walter Keeping. He's a teacher who made a difference. He's cool and enthusiastic, and he was the start of my wanting to learn. He always has a story to tell, and those stories have stuck with me. He inspired me to reach my potential, including getting fit.

Lorri Allen and Larry Estepa, the hosts of *Mornings with Lorri and Larry.* They provided me with the opportunity to do my first live television appearance and helped me realize that people would be interested in how I lost weight. Lorri and her husband, Mark, helped me learn to share my story with the media and with small groups. They've been a fantastic help and encouragement.

The great products available now to help us eat healthy: Healthy Choice dinners, Special K cereal and crackers, Nature Valley granola bars, and Egg Beaters. Our family travels at top speed all day, and it's good to have fast, healthy alternatives to gooey snacks and drive-thru meals. And I'm especially grateful for my super treat, my I-never-feel-deprived gourmet dessert: Coca-Cola Zero.

Bob and Ruth Hall, topnotch editors and family friends. They gave me the gift of their time and expertise as we put the finishing touches on this book.

My phenomenal agent, Claire Gerus. When I learned that someone as experienced and talented as Claire was interested in my book, I was hopeful that my fitness plan could help others.

Health Communications, Inc. (HCI) and the topnotch team that made this book possible. One of the best things Claire did was to connect me with just the right publisher. HCI chooses to publish books that change lives, and that's what I hope this book does. Special thanks to my editor, Carol Rosenberg, who strengthened the book without changing my message.

At the end of a day, I'm satisfied when I've had all the necessary vitamins, minerals, and other nutrients—in the right quantities and proportions. I know that's a big step toward a healthy lifestyle. And I'm just as satisfied, at the end of the day, when I think about all the people who touch my life and have a part in helping me reach my potential. They're the components that keep me fit and healthy and ready to face my new thin life. Thank you, family, friends, and other special people!

—Taylor LeBaron

Introduction

A TALE OF TWO BOYS

This is the story of two boys.

The first boy had a DNA code that made him prone to being overweight. His natural build, coupled with his stationary hobbies and junk-food cravings, caused his weight to soar to nearly 300. Even as a preteen, he had trouble finding clothes to fit. He got winded after just a few minutes of walking, so running and other sports were out of the question.

He took some good-natured teasing about his weight. Once, as he changed after gym class, a boy shouted, "Whoa, dude. You need a bra." The other kids roared.

"Whatever," replied the boy, pushing the comment to a deep recess of his mind where it wouldn't hurt.

The boy knew his weight was a serious problem, and he avoided scales. By his early teens, he worried about cholesterol, diabetes, and high blood pressure. He avoided amusement parks because he was over the weight limit for most rides. He slept in his jeans so they would be loose enough to wear to school.

The other boy was thin and agile. He sat cross-legged on the floor and scrambled up trees with ease. At nearly six feet tall, he tucked his size-small shirt into his skinny jeans with the 30-inch waist, fastened his belt with a buckle that said BUILT FORD TOUGH, and attacked each day with enthusiasm and confidence.

This boy could run five or six miles at full speed without a break. His biggest worry was getting his heart rate up high enough to get a good workout during his almost-daily trips to the gym.

The kids at school knew he was tough, and one day, a boy who outweighed him challenged him to arm wrestle. When the boy won, the other kids asked him to flex his muscles.

"Dude, you're strong," said another kid.

"Yeah, whatever," replied the boy, making light of the compliment but storing it in the deep recess of his mind where he could replay it later.

This is the story of two boys. The trouble was that one boy was inside the other.

—Jack and Mary Branson

Part One

Answering the Call of Fitness

Growing Up Chunky

My favorite TV show has always been the old *Dukes of Hazzard* series, and I often dreamed of being like Bo Duke. John Schneider, who played the part, was thin and agile. He never used the door of his car, the General Lee. He just jumped in through the window. He hoisted himself up with his arms, slid his legs through the window of the General Lee, and—voilà!— he was ready to ride.

One day, I decided to duplicate Bo's stunt. Somehow, I raised myself up and got my legs through the window of Mom's car. But my body was too big to fit through the window. I was stuck— too big to slide into the car and too far in to get out safely. The only way out was to fall, so I tumbled into a heap on the driveway, hoping none of the neighbors saw me. The stunt I'd planned for fun turned out to be one of my worst "fat" memories.

I can talk about my fat memories now, but for a long time I couldn't think of myself as fat, and I refused to see my size as a problem, especially *my* problem.

I told myself it was my binary code. I was designed to be big. It was my natural build. After all, I was a big baby—9 pounds,

4 ounces—and a sturdy toddler. By elementary school, I was always one of the biggest kids in my class.

At the beginning of each school year, I would try to scout out a kid of equal or bigger size to boost my confidence. That way, I could tell myself I wasn't the only big kid in the class. When I couldn't find someone my size, I knew I'd take all the ribbing that year. If there was another fat kid, I knew they could take the fall with me. I could share the insults.

If you're reading this book, you may have some unpleasant fat memories of your own. If so, you can probably relate to the physical and emotional challenges behind my memories. Follow me through a few more memories, and you'll realize that I understand where you are because I've been there.

Then follow me through the rest of the book as I describe how I faced my obesity and how I changed my life by changing my weight. I hope that soon you'll relate to all segments of this book: living with obesity, deciding to get fit, developing and carrying out a plan, and experiencing a new and exciting life in a thin, healthy body. Read on.

MY FAT MEMORIES

On field day at the end of first grade, the teachers announced that one of the games would be tug of war. As we ate lunch, the kids argued over whose side I would be on.

"We'll win if we have Taylor," one kid said.

I was big, and they assumed I was tough. It felt great. But when it came time for tug of war, my size just got in the way, and I wasn't as strong as the wiry kids. Our team lost.

In third grade, I remember the kids talking about how much

they weighed. A kid pointed to me and said, "*He* probably weighs over 100." I did. I weighed 130.

By sixth grade, my weight was snowballing. On the last day of school, I dropped a book. When I bent over to pick it up, the extra flesh on my face hung down.

One of the kids standing nearby said, "Look at Taylor. He's got a double chin."

Everybody laughed, including me. But I felt an actual physical reaction to the humiliation: my arms and legs tingled, and my face flushed. And here I am, years later, remembering what the room was like, what the kid said, and exactly how I felt. Words hurt.

That kid probably forgot his words as soon as he said them, but every word stuck with me. The jokes and insults about my weight were like burrs that you get when you walk through a thicket. You keep walking and shaking your legs to get rid of them. But the more you walk, the more burrs stick to you. The more I walked through life with insults sticking to me, the harder they were to shake.

My Highest Weight

The summer before seventh grade, my great-grandmother died. Our family went to Kentucky for the funeral, and I refused to dress up. I loved my great-grandmother and I wanted to look good and show respect for her at the funeral, but I knew the only clothes that fit without strain were huge jeans—rolled up multiple times—and a stretched-out 2X T-shirt, not tucked in.

Before the funeral, we stopped at my other great-grandmother's. I was alone in her apartment and decided to weigh myself. I carried the scale into her kitchen, on a flat surface, so I could get an accurate weight. It had been a while since I'd been weighed at the doctor's so I had no idea what to expect. But I wasn't prepared for what I read on my great-grandmother's scale: 297.

My Biggest Eye Openers

By seventh grade, classroom desks were a problem. I attended a small private school with just a few desks in each room. Usually one desk near the back of the room had a separate chair. The others were typical kid desks with chairs attached. I found the biggest desk in each classroom and tried to stake it out as mine. But sometimes, if I didn't get to class early, someone else would grab the big desk, and I'd be packed into a small one. I'd spend the next fifty minutes in agony, unable to take a deep breath or turn from side to side. Then I'd have to squeeze myself out when the bell rang. Hours later, I'd still have a deep red mark across my stomach where the desk had cut into the skin.

One afternoon, our class took on a project to clear the nature trails around our school. It felt weird to see the other kids walking and laughing and skipping, because just a few minutes into the work, I was dying. My calves ached unbearably, and I nearly passed out. The whole team—students and teachers—had to stop to help me. They got me some water and everyone crowded around, wondering if I could finish the project. I slowed down the entire team, and I'm sure the other kids secretly resented me.

No one said much to me during the rest of the project. They

didn't have to. I was saying plenty to myself. I was telling myself that I wasn't carrying my load on the team, that there were certain things I couldn't do and probably would never be able to do. I was sure I'd never be an athlete. I couldn't be a police officer or join the military. I'd never be John Schneider's stunt double.

Even though I was angry at myself for slowing the team down—and even though I knew my future options were limited— I wouldn't fully admit that my weight was a problem. Half the time, I would think: *I'm big, I'm strong.* Other times, I would feel fat. When I told myself that I was just big, the confidence didn't last long. Someone usually made sure I knew I was fat.

Other kids would make fun of me—not on a regular basis, but it happened. They'd be climbing on gym equipment or sitting on a table, and someone would say, "Don't let Taylor on that. He'll break it." I'd laugh with the others, but I'd feel that familiar tingling and flushing.

In spite of the occasional insult, I wanted friends, and being overweight separated me socially—and even physically—from the other kids. When our class took field trips, the kids would banter and bond with the kids they sat beside on the bus. But no one wanted to sit beside me because there wasn't enough room. I'd try to scrunch up against the window, but the seat next to me was always the last seat chosen. To make room for someone to sit beside me, I'd have to press my legs against each other so hard that they'd go numb.

Each year, I grew larger. My eating habits combined with my DNA to create a big guy who was quickly outgrowing his environment. Chairs mysteriously broke at our house. Not occasionally, but regularly. We eventually needed all new dining room chairs.

When my brother and I got new bedroom furniture, we both wanted bunk beds. We settled on two regular full-size beds because the bunk beds we wanted had a 200-pound weight limit.

My Greatest Challenges

I always loved carbs, and when I was twelve and thirteen, I had cheese grits and cheese biscuits nearly every morning. Occasionally, I'd vary my breakfast menu by having a tall stack of pancakes drowning in syrup. Mom sometimes used liquid diet drinks as meal replacements, and when I saw them in the pantry, I'd grab one to wash down a snack.

I ate a lot, and almost always the wrong things. I didn't *think* I ate out of stress, but I knew I ate without realizing it. I just ate whatever, whenever. I ate while watching TV, and it was pretty standard to down three or four flavored milk drinks and half a dozen snack cakes while watching reruns of the Duke boys and the General Lee speeding through Hazzard County. Since I didn't think about what I was eating, I didn't feel full until I was stuffed. I ate "whatever" until I felt cramped.

I studied health in school, and I knew how to eat well. I just didn't do it. And it wasn't like good food wasn't all around me. But I ignored the fruit bowl and stayed friendly with the cookie jar. I ate whatever I wanted in whatever quantities it took to give me that stuffed feeling.

My brother, Elliott, was naturally skinny, and he ate more junk than I did. It didn't seem fair that I had inherited the fat gene, so I told myself that I deserved to eat what I wanted, too.

Mom wanted to lose weight, but every time she mentioned it, I went ballistic. I've never liked change, and she thought that was the reason for my resistance to her getting healthy. The truth was, I didn't want Mom to lose because I couldn't. In the back of my mind, I was thinking, *If I can't do it, I don't want anyone else to.*

My Limitations

I liked being the first to get the mail each day, and I still do. I wanted to sort through the stacks to find my tech magazines and the computer gadgets I ordered, and to check for that elusive, long-awaited personal letter from Bill Gates. I couldn't trust the rest of the family with such valuable correspondence, so as soon as I heard the mail truck in front of our house, I was out the door.

Grabbing the mail was a cinch. Our house has a driveway that makes the Grand Canyon look level. You can almost roll down to the mailbox. But when I got to the bottom, envelopes and magazines in hand, and stared up at the climb, I'd start to sweat just thinking of it. By the time I lugged myself back to the house, my heart was racing and my shirt was soaked.

I stayed away from scales except for doctors' visits, so each time I got weighed, I was jolted by a much bigger number. As my weight climbed, theme parks became a challenge. Too many rides had weight limits. Some 220, some 250. As I stood in line with my friends, I worried that the ride attendant would refuse to let me on the ride (humiliation). I worried that the attendant would let me on the ride but I wouldn't be able to fasten the safety belt (devastation). And I worried that I'd fasten the safety belt but my weight would cause the ride to wreck (death and disaster). After telling friends too many times that I'd "changed my mind," and backtracking through the long line for the roller coaster, I decided theme parks weren't for me.

I wanted to try bungee jumping at a sporting goods store at the mall, but I was above the weight limit. I didn't need the attendant to tell me I was too big to bungee jump. The thought of snapping the cable and landing on my head was enough to keep me out of the line.

School activities were the worst because they were mandatory. I couldn't turn around, change my mind, or avoid the activity altogether. I nearly passed out one hot Georgia afternoon when our class did the 20-yard dash. For me, it was more of a never-ending crawl.

My teachers were understanding when I had to stop to catch my breath after just ten minutes of a nature walk, but I could tell that the other kids thought I'd brought it on myself.

Some of the things average-weight kids take for granted were a chore for me. Taking a bath took me twice as long because my body mass took up so much of the tub that I couldn't fill it with enough water to get clean. Halfway through my bath, I had to let out the water and refill the tub.

I needed 3X T-shirts, but they were hard to find. To make a 2X fit, I'd lay it on the bed and reach my arms between the top and bottom layers. Then I'd pull my arms as far apart as I could, stretching the fabric to the max. Sometimes, when I saw the stretched shirt lying on my bed, I'd think, *My shirt is big enough to cover the grill of a Mack truck*.

I needed size-44 jeans, but we could only find two pairs. When I had to wear 42s, I'd lie on the bed to fasten them at night, then sleep in them so they'd be loose enough to wear to school the next day.

Sometimes the things that embarrassed me most were things

others probably didn't notice. It was humiliating to buy a shirt and have the clerk get my size from a special drawer below the "regular" sizes. I didn't have to special-order my clothes, but shopping wasn't any fun. I'd always had trouble finding pants that fit. When I was in elementary school, even husky jeans didn't fit, so I usually wore sweatpants. As I got older, I often found that the biggest jeans in a store were still too small. And when I found some that fit in the waist, I had to roll up the pants legs three or four times.

My Biggest Fears

I dodged the doctor's office because that's where I had to face my weight. When Dr. Bagheri brought out the growth chart, I could feel my hands tremble. Each time he showed me my weight in relation to other kids my age, I was off the charts.

I insisted on over-the-counter medicine whenever possible to avoid seeing the doctor. I didn't want blood work done because I was terrified that my cholesterol was higher than my weight. I knew obesity contributed to all sorts of health problems—no one had to tell me.

I think Dr. Bagheri understood that. Except for showing me the growth chart, he didn't pressure or embarrass me. It was the nurses who went on and on about my weight. And some of them were overweight, too.

My Major Awareness

In eighth grade, our class took a field trip to Stone Mountain, one of Georgia's famous landmarks—a mountain carved with a Confederate scene of Robert E. Lee, Jefferson Davis, and

Stonewall Jackson. A bunch of the guys decided to check out the trail to the top of the mountain, so I went with them. I saw younger and older people climbing, but I knew I'd never make it to the top. I was relieved when our teacher said we didn't have time to climb the mountain that day. He promised we'd plan another field trip just for the climb. I knew then that I'd opt out of the second trip.

I look back now at photos of myself at twelve, thirteen, and fourteen, and there's no denying I was fat. But I rarely thought of myself that way. In my mind, I was just a big guy. At fourteen, I was 5'11", so weighing more than 200 pounds didn't seem so bad. I just never let myself think about how much above 200 I'd climbed.

I thought about myself like a rugged Mack truck. I enjoyed wearing a T-shirt that said "Built Ford Tough." But most of the time I couldn't live up to that description. In fact, "tough" and "me" were on opposite ends of the spectrum. I couldn't walk far without getting out of breath, and whatever school team I was on usually came in last because I couldn't keep up.

But on that field trip to Stone Mountain, I finally admitted to myself that I wasn't just a big guy. I was a *really, really* big guy who was *really, really* out of shape. I needed only about half the body weight I was carrying around, and the extra weight was affecting my life as much as a virus affects a computer.

My Greatest Advantage

Despite my weight, life was still a blast. I had a knack for computers, so at thirteen I started my own web-design business. My family laughed a lot, did things together, and created fun out of even ordinary days. Being Taylor was overall good.

But when things were *extra* great, I couldn't even jump for joy. Jumping up and down hurt my legs. I felt plenty of joy in my heart, but my weight kept me from showing it.

For several years, I had a recurring dream. It was so vivid that I'd wake up feeling exhilarated. I dreamed I met some sort of fairy godmother, like the one in the Cinderella story, and she gave me three wishes. I asked for $10 million. I asked for a replica of the General Lee. And I said I wanted to weigh 180 pounds.

What I didn't realize is that I didn't need a fairy godmother to make my last wish come true. . . .

2

Fighting Back

The more I thought about my weight problem, the more I knew I couldn't totally blame my binary code. Binary code could be rewritten. I could retrain myself and rewrite my future. A really old comic strip character, Pogo, once said: "I saw the enemy, and he is us." That sure fit me as I started looking for reasons I was overweight. I could do a lot to counteract the build I had inherited instead of giving up. The first thing I did was identify what was putting on the pounds. Since I love video games, I approached my weight issue the same way I learn a new game. When I get a new video game, one of the first things I do is check out the opponents to see what I'm up against. When I know the enemies, I can create a plan of attack.

ENEMY #1: STILL LIFE

My first problem was inactivity. I put calories in, but I expended very little energy to burn them. So I decided to exercise. I rode my bike once around our cul-de-sac, and I was exhausted. When I didn't see a difference right away, I gave up. I wasn't ready to face the activity issue yet.

ENEMY #2: TRICKY TASTE BUDS

On to the next challenge: food choices. For my whole life, I'd let my taste buds lead me instead of my brain. And I was coming to the realization that my taste buds were not my friends. They were out for themselves, regardless of what they did to me. They told me that flavored whole milk drinks, nougat candy bars, tortilla chips, packaged dessert cakes, and regular soft drinks had a place in my life. But when I started checking out the makeup of these foods, I realized they shouldn't even be classified as foods. They were pleasure for my mouth but torture for my body.

So I told myself: *I'll lose weight this week. I'll cut out all the junk. And to hurry the process, I'll even skip lunch.*

But the junk cravings didn't go away. In fact, they got stronger. And when I skipped lunch, I was so hungry by supper that I had double servings.

ENEMY #3: SNEAKY SERVINGS

My last hope: food volume. When I first investigated what I put into my mouth, I realized I had no idea what a serving size was. After a few days of measuring, I realized that my soup bowl of cereal held four or five servings and, depending on the type of cereal, could be as much as 1,000 calories, not counting milk.

ENEMY #4: BIG LITTLE THINGS

I soon learned that I could easily consume my day's calories in liquids. Liquid calories are more likely to make you gain weight because after you drink them, even if you feel full, your mind tells you that you haven't had a meal. I knew I had to give up flavored milk drinks and regular soft drinks. I figured if that was the only change I made, I'd lose a little weight.

I realized that condiments were a big calorie waste for me, too. I loved a giant cheeseburger with mayonnaise and ketchup oozing down the sides. I could save a couple of hundred calories just by vetoing the mayo (180 calories for 2 tablespoons) and ketchup (30 calories for 2 tablespoons).

ENEMY #5: STRESS IN ALL SIZES

I had more to consider than exercise, food choices, and serving sizes. I had to realize why I overate, and the reason became clear when I thought back to when I was twelve. In a little over two years, I'd experienced some unbelievable stressors that skyrocketed me from chubby kid to obese teen. I'll tell you more about these in Chapter 5, but trust me, these were *major* stressors.

But stress is stress, and even minor, everyday stressors can cause overeating. Stress of all types caused me to eat mindlessly until my stomach shouted, "We're full down here!" and not another bite would fit. I called it "whatever" eating, and I knew I had to avoid whatever eating at whatever cost.

Toward the end of this major stress time, my granddad bought me my first laptop. I loved surfing the Internet, and one day I found a health site with a huge headline that read: HOW DO YOU KNOW IF YOU'RE OVERWEIGHT?

I keyed in my height and a weight estimate, which I knew was probably lower than my actual weight. The calculation came back: MORBIDLY OBESE. The label hurt and panicked me. The image of Taylor LeBaron as morbidly obese was getting too clear to deny. . . .

WHAT NOW?

I knew why I was obese.

→ **I was eating *too much* of the *wrong* foods.**

→ **I was spending too many hours in front of the TV and computer—in other words, not getting enough exercise.**

Once I figured out what I was doing wrong, you'd think I'd start doing what I knew was right. But it wasn't that easy. The decision to shape up was a slow process for me. But I began by paying a little more attention to what I ate, and I eliminated flavored milk drinks and regular soft drinks from my diet.

As for exercise? Well, on the few occasions when I lifted something heavy or did short exercises at school, I liked the way it made me feel. I could feel my muscles, and I enjoyed it. But I rarely exercised, and it didn't stick.

The Gift

The Christmas just after I turned fourteen, my grandparents gave my family a membership to our local YMCA. Even though I was a little more health conscious, I remember thinking it was a lame gift, and I wanted no part of it. Mom was excited, though, and early in January, she took Elliott and me to check out the YMCA and to get our ID cards.

To be honest, when I looked at all those people grunting and sweating and working hard—running on treadmills and going nowhere—I thought it was a joke. Exercise couldn't possibly make *that* much difference. Our Y membership sat for two months.

Then, in March, Mom suggested that we all set fitness goals. I was not a fan of the idea and didn't want to go back to the Y. I felt self-conscious. All the people there seemed so fit and healthy, and I doubted my physical ability. I figured there would be very little I could do. But at Mom's insistence, we made our second trip to the Y.

The Coach

The Y assigned me a personal trainer, a fit and trim lady named Dyan. She started out with a physical assessment, and I was pleased that my weight was down to 282. (Those little changes in my diet had made a difference.) Dyan didn't make me feel bad about myself. We just sat for a while talking about my weight, what I ate, and what my goals were. I didn't tell her my mom had pretty much dragged me there or that I was self-conscious and embarrassed to be discussing my weight, activity level, and eating habits with such a lean and fit person.

Dyan seemed so different from me. And as I looked around, I realized how different I was from all the people working out, running track, and swimming. I didn't think I belonged in their world. My lifestyle was too different. But then Dyan showed me pictures of her that had been taken a couple of years earlier. She was my size! She told me how she'd exercised and watched her diet and eventually saw huge changes. I listened politely, but I found it hard to believe her. *She must have had liposuction or taken diet pills to have lost that much weight,* I thought.

Dyan went on to say that a fitness program would be a life-changing experience, but I couldn't see how that was possible. I was ready to give up before I started. She said that 90 percent of people who make New Year's resolutions to lose weight give up within eight weeks, but that I didn't have to be one of them. (Secretly, I figured my odds were worse because Mom had made the resolution for me.)

Dyan went over what exercises would be safe for me. She started me out on a few of the weight machines, a stationary bike, and a treadmill. Within ten minutes on the stationary bike, my pulse was up to 190, and I had to stop. I was too big to run and could crack my kneecaps, so I was only able to walk slowly on the treadmill.

Dyan and I met weekly to talk about my fitness strategy. She taught me how to read and understand food labels. She taught me about calorie values, about fat, saturated fat, and trans fats, and how muscles are built and how they deteriorate. She explained body mass index (BMI), which is a measurement of your body fat based on height and weight. She also explained basal metabolic rate (BMR), which is the amount of calories you'd burn if you stayed in bed all day. All this information just made me realize how out of shape I was.

I'd gone far enough that I didn't want to back out. But I felt like all the healthy, thin people would be staring at me. I didn't want them to see the size of my legs. I didn't want them to see me at all. So I showed up the first time wearing sunglasses, jeans, and boots. These clothes became my workout gear for the next several months. I didn't realize at the time that my clothing made me even more noticeable.

The Progress

I started out slow, but I stuck with it. I didn't notice a weight loss right away, but after just a week, I started feeling that natural high people talk about. Exercise exhilarated me. I felt like I'd found something I was always meant to do. I felt my muscles getting stronger every day. I began going to the Y four, five, or even six days a week. I began feeling like a character in one of my video games: facing enemies, maneuvering around obstacles, moving to a higher level each time I mastered the current one. I began feeling powerful.

It wasn't long before I *had* to go to the Y, and I became upset if, for some reason, I wasn't able to go. Exercise quickly became a part of what I did each day, and I found simpler ways to exercise on days I couldn't go to the Y. Exercise became my replacement for snacking and my remedy for stress. I felt happy if I was sweating and grunting like the people I once thought were foolish.

After a couple of months, Dyan could tell a difference, but she was the only one. The weight didn't come off fast, but I was changing my lifestyle. And my diet began to naturally change. After working out for an hour, brownies and snack cakes didn't sound as good as a bottle of cold energy water. And I knew I needed the whole fitness program if I wanted to see results, so I started changing what I ate.

At first I thought that I could just count fat and that as long as my diet had less than 65 grams of fat a day, I'd lose weight.

I soon realized that those fat grams couldn't come in the form of candy bars and snack cakes because they were packed with calories. Those calories were empty, and I knew I needed protein for my workouts.

I spent a lot of time searching the Internet and visiting websites. I typed in questions like "How many calories does a beef burrito have?" and "What is a serving size for steak?" I visited fast-food sites and identified the healthiest foods on every menu so I'd have a good alternative for the high-calorie, high-fat, high-sugar items I'd ordered in the past. For a while, I used an online site to plan my meals and keep track of what I ate. (You can find a great online meal planner at www.health vault.com.) Eventually, I developed a healthy diet and exercise plan that worked for me, and I no longer needed the site.

I tackled fitness with three strategies:

1. Increased physical activity
2. Decreased food volume
3. Healthy food choices

The YMCA provided computerized exercise plans, so I could watch my progress. They used an incentive program called the Coach Approach that helped me chart my progress as I reached different color levels, much like karate belts. I even earned prizes like wristbands, T-shirts, and gym bags.

By the time summer arrived, I was driven to exercise. I was starting a new school in the fall, and I wanted to be in shape. I worked out two to three hours at a time. I knew I couldn't keep up that pace after school started, but I wanted a jumpstart. I'd finish the workout Dyan designed for me, walk a mile or two around the track, and repeat my workout plan. I felt myself getting stronger from the inside out. I was still a big guy, but I was starting to feel and act like the person I'd always known I was.

It was easier to control food volume when I paid attention to what I ate. I started noticing everything I put in my mouth—the nutritional value and the serving size. I realized I didn't need a big bowl of anything to get the necessary vitamins and minerals, but I was still so large that I needed a lot of calories. I reduced my daily calories slowly because I didn't want to lose weight so fast that my skin sagged.

The Cravings

The hardest thing about food choices was dealing with cravings. I decided that cravings were sort of like dinosaurs. If they lost their food supply, they'd die. So I stopped feeding my cravings. I knew a lot of people learned to satisfy their cravings with a bite of cake instead of a wedge, and I did that sometimes, too. But my cravings were pushy. If I fed them too often, even tiny bites, they tried to take over.

Every time I felt a craving, I'd work out or jump into an activity I enjoyed. Mom bought me some 20-pound barbells to use for quick workouts at home. I decided it was better for me to lift weights while I watched television than to snack.

Eventually, the cravings started to die, and I'd wake up in the morning and want salmon or other protein. I'd feel hungry for whole-grain bread instead of a muffin. Finally, I was stronger than my cravings.

FITNESS 101

I approached my diet like I tackled a major school research project. I learned about every food ingredient. I researched what I needed to be healthy, and I compared what I needed with what was on food labels. I started going to the store with Mom so I could read labels and choose the healthiest foods. As I developed my own system, I became more focused on carrying out the plan than on feeding my taste buds.

I started liking healthy foods, and after a while, rich foods made me queasy. I was truly changing my inner codes. I was now controlling my taste buds instead of letting them control me. That powerful feeling felt better than any food could ever taste!

3

Playing THE ULTIMATE FITNESS GAME (UFG)

I'm a techie guy, and I love everything about computers and electronics. When I started my exercise program, I was playing a lot of military games on my PlayStation. So when I came across Marine Corps cadences at www.militaryrecordings.com, they were the perfect accompaniment to my exercise program. I purchased two Marine Corps cadence CDs and downloaded them onto my Zune and let them take me to boot camp five or six times a week. (There's a Marine Corps cadence CD for women, too.) I loved the beat, and I listened to the messages: *Go strong! Don't give up! Endure!*

I discovered that I was a natural for Marine tactics. The cadences did more for me than the double workouts I'd done over the summer. I would like to thank the U.S. Marine Corps for my increase in speed and endurance. The cadences helped me run faster and longer. I repeated the messages back in my mind as I ran at full speed on the treadmill: *One mile, no sweat. Two miles, no good. Three miles, we're going strong. Four miles, we're almost there. Five miles, we're going home.*

I felt like I was training alongside the Marines, listening to the sound of boots hitting the ground and dog tags jingling.

Wearing my own dog tags tucked under my shirt, I imagined I was running at Parris Island instead of the Forsyth County, Georgia, YMCA. The cadences kept me disciplined and inspired. If I could keep up with Marine training, even if just on the CDs, I felt I'd accomplished something pretty great for a boy who, a year ago, couldn't run a 20-yard dash.

I still wear dog tags when I work out, and I still listen to cadences. When I feel like I can't go any farther, I crank up the volume and let the Marines tell me I can.

I tackled the physical part of my fitness program by turning my training over to the Marines. I let the cadences motivate me as I followed the YMCA's exercise plan. The more I worked out, the more calories I burned. It actually became fun. And without realizing it, I began approaching fitness just like I played a video game. I called my approach the ULTIMATE FITNESS GAME.

THE ULTIMATE FITNESS GAME (UFG)

In most video games, you follow a path and confront obstacles along the way. Dangers lurk in dark, narrow corridors. You enter a room and everything you click on offers you a choice. And there's always something you run out of: ammo, money, energy, stamina, health. I play UFG like calories are the money that I'll run out of if I don't spend wisely.

I follow a road through my day, and I have a choice of transportation, just like I'd have in a video game. I can run down the road and increase my skill level, or I can hop in a car and drive. Every time I decide to walk or run, I add money to my account because I'm burning more calories.

Obstacles are everywhere. Each room I enter offers choices. In the kitchen and the school lunchroom, all sorts of "dangerous" foods loom out at me. They look good, but they have high price tags and do nothing to advance me in UFG. In fact, they fight against fitness. I have to make my money last all day and cover my necessary expenses, so I can't be tricked into buying dangerous foods. They're the enemy.

The Money

Each morning, I calculate how much "money" I have to spend for that day—one dollar for every calorie I'll burn. I know that my BMR is 1,850. (That's the amount of calories I'd burn if I did *nothing* all day. You can find BMR calculators on a lot of Internet sites.) I know I'll burn a couple of hundred more calories just working at my computer, talking, walking to class, and doing normal stuff. And I know that my body will burn an extra 10 percent of the calories I consume just to digest my food. So if I'm sick in bed with a cold, I still have more than $2,000 to spend without gaining weight. For all other days, I factor in my exercise to determine my "salary" for the day.

I usually take a break from the Y on Saturday and just hang out with friends, see a movie, or work on my computer. I figure I can safely spend $2,000 on lazy Saturdays. My weekend treat is usually a 12-inch plain meat sub, so I know I'll spend $600 for supper. That leaves me $1,400 for the rest of the day. As soon as I wake up and determine my salary for the day, I start planning how to spend it. And I keep a running count all day so my money lasts the full sixteen hours I'm awake. I like math, so I figure everything in my head. But most cell phones and computers have calculators, so anyone can keep track of calories.

I know that on a no-exercise day I'm on a tight budget, so just like I was shopping on a budget, I look for bargains. If I can find a two-for-one sale, that helps me stretch my budget. I can buy two pieces of whole-grain bread for $50 each instead of one piece of regular bread for $100.

One frosted cupcake may cost $350, so I can't afford that kind of splurge too often. I have bills to pay: meat, milk, fruit, veggies, and whole grains. These foods are like my basic house and car payments, insurance, and utilities. Until I pay them, I'd be irresponsible to spend my money on luxuries. The basic foods are where I get my energy. If I don't pay for them first, I'll run out of energy before I run out of day.

I consider snack treats like my real-life movie budget. Since I'm on a tight budget and don't have much money to go to the movies, I may be able to go only once a month. When I realize that my favorite candy bar will cost me $230, I know I will rarely have the money to buy a candy bar.

On days I go to the Y, I feel like I got a big sales bonus at work and I have more money to spend. I know that just forty-five minutes of free weights will burn about 350 calories, so on days when I know I'm going to do free weights, I add $350 to my starting budget. On a regular busy day with exercise, I start my day with $2,500 to $2,600.

That's more than enough if I play the game right. But if enemy foods lure me into spending too much of my money, I'll end up broke too early and **GAME OVER** will print across the day's screen. Then I'll have long hours that night with no money left to buy food.

The Obstacles

It would be easier to spend my money wisely if I lived in a vacuum, but as I travel through the day playing UFG, there's always danger of a lag. People enter the road from narrow paths, and the game can get congested. Some offer me chips and milkshakes. Others offer steamed veggies and high-protein snacks. Each time someone offers me something, I have to make a decision—a decision I live with for the rest of the day.

Now that I've lost weight, some people say, "You're *too* thin. You need to eat." Or "One cookie won't hurt you." Friends and family mean well, but each time they offer me an off-limits food, they're sabotaging my strategy. So I turn around and run, just the way I'd take another path to avoid an enemy in a game.

The object of UFG is to get down the road and through the maze of rooms without running out of money. At night, I can save the game and start again the next day. I get to keep my overall score (my weight loss), but I start each morning with a new budget for that day.

The Big Win

Some games have only one winner, but not UFG. It's more like the video games where you're the only player. You compete against yourself and you try to beat your own best score, to do better than the day before. Everyone can play, and everyone can win.

I call it the Ultimate Fitness Game because the prize is a whole new lifestyle. At the end of the game, you peel back the fat suit you've been hiding behind and you show the world the amazing person who's been there all along. It's sort of like letting the superhero take off his disguise after he fights all the bad guys. Now the world knows your true identity. You introduce the world to the person you've always been.

The Strategy

The hardest parts of the game are figuring out the strategy and getting started. A video game comes with a game guide, and you have basic rules to follow, but you eventually develop your own game strategy. It's the same with UFG. I can tell you the basics, but in the end, you have to develop a personal strategy that works for you.

And the best way to get started is to tackle fitness a little at a time. When you play a video game, you don't worry about the whole game at the same time. You start down a corridor and worry only about the dangers in that part of the game. You have to do that in UFG, too. If you don't, the game will seem overwhelming and you'll quit on the first screen.

The Climb

I remember how hopeless I felt when I knew I had more than 100 pounds to lose. It was like looking down a long road that I couldn't see the end of. Somewhere way down past the trees and the rocks and the turns in the road, a treasure might be waiting for me. But I couldn't see the prize, so it didn't seem real. I had to learn to divide my large goal of losing 100 pounds into smaller goals and face the small ones head on.

When I first started working out and eating right, I felt like I had just been belted into a roller coaster. I could hear the gears clacking, and I was on a steep climb. It was scary, but I told myself it was too late to get off. For a long time, it was a slow uphill ride. I worked out and no one noticed the difference. I totally changed my diet, and even I didn't feel much thinner.

But just like when you reach the top of a roller coaster and start dropping so fast that you feel like your stomach is in your throat, I reached a peak in the program. All of a sudden my pants size started dropping, and I felt like the weight was melting off. And the thrill was worth the long upward climb.

The Choices

As I started the long climb to a new lifestyle, I found that eliminating choices helped me eat right. The fewer choices I had to make, the easier it was to stick to my routine.

I eventually developed a basic diet that continues to work for me. There's enough variation to make eating enjoyable, but it's so regimented that I never have to ask myself, "Should I have a piece of cake? Do I want a bedtime snack?" Those options aren't included in my routine.

And I don't have to ask myself whether I'll work out. Exercise is no longer a choice. It's as much a part of my daily routine as brushing my teeth. My routine varies according to the busyness of the day, but I always exercise. Some days I do cardio, and some days—if I'm extra-tired, stay late at school, or have an evening activity—I don't. But some sort of workout is nonnegotiable.

The Schedule

This has been my typical day for more than two years:

My alarm goes off at 5:20 AM. I know I'm starting a new phase of **UFG**, so I calculate my "salary" for the day. Usually it's about $2,500, or 2,500 calories. When that's gone, it's gone.

With the day's budget established, I go to the kitchen and grab a handful of low-sugar whole-grain cereal. I can now easily judge a three-quarter cup serving size. I pour half a cup of milk into the cereal (I can now visually measure my milk serving). I add a fat-free or low-fat/low-sugar pro-digestive yogurt, and breakfast is served.

At school, I'm involved in a program that lets me do a lot of walking around campus. My stomach is gnawing a little by midmorning, so during my 10:20 break, I have an oats and honey granola bar. That sustains me till lunch.

Our school has no cafeteria, so lunch is catered from local fast-food restaurants. One day, they bring in pizza, another day Mexican, and so on. Those are choices I can't afford. Since we have microwaves in our eating area, I bring a Healthy Choice dinner for lunch. That way, I make my choices among the variety of portion-controlled dinners instead of choosing whether I'll have one or two slices of pizza. I have a bottle of water with lunch, and my major treat is always a Coke Zero.

If I have an extra snack for lunch, I do the math and know what to eliminate later in the day. And an "extra snack" is never junk. If someone brings cupcakes or cookies to school for a birthday, I just say no thanks. I can enjoy celebrating with my friends without messing up the running score I'm keeping for **UFG**.

By the time the school bell rings at 3:00 PM, I'm famished. I have three slices of lean turkey on two slices of whole-grain bread—no mayonnaise or other condiments, and no cheese. As we drive to the Y, I eat a low-sugar meal-replacement protein bar. I choose the ones with 28–32 grams of protein because I know I'll need energy for my workout.

By now, I've probably had 1,450 calories. It may sound extreme for me to be so exact, but I know what I eat. I'm aware. It's all part of **UFG**, so I keep tallying my score throughout the day.

It's not just a matter of resisting enemy foods; part of the strategy is choosing the right foods. Each time I buy protein or other important nutrients, I increase my energy score, just like when you pick up new weapons and prizes as you play a video game. Instead of concentrating on taste sensations, I'm focusing on what I need for energy. I know I have only a certain amount of money to spend, and I use strategy to spend it wisely. If I want to have strength for my workout, I have to buy foods that provide energy, and I have to keep my spending within my budget.

At the Y, I do 45–55 minutes of physical training. I start with the machines that tone various parts of my body. Then I do free-weight arm curls, bench presses, leg presses, ab crunches, chest presses, and end with time on a rowing machine.

Then I hop onto the treadmill. I run one to five miles, depending on how much time we have. Five miles adds forty or so minutes to the workout, but if we have time, I love it. It's my stress reliever. If I feel angry about something, I run longer. I also do the stair climber, the elliptical, and other heavy workout machines.

As soon as I progressed to free weights, they became most important. Free weights do more for overall fitness than weight machines, treadmills, and ellipticals and burn just as many calories. They've definitely become the favorite part of my workout.

Until you get some experience, weight machines are safer and more effective than free weights. You can set machines to the exact amount of weight you want to use, you can adjust the seat height, and you can follow clear instructions on how to use them (usually posted on the machines). And most important, you don't have to worry about dropping the weights.

The problem with weight machines is that the machines cause your movements to be so smooth that the lifting is a little easier and you don't get quite as tough a workout as you get with free weights. And if you position your body certain ways on most machines, you can "cheat" by moving just enough to register a repetition but not enough to work your muscles.

Free weights definitely give you a tougher workout, but they're not for beginners. They can be dangerous if you drop them, and you can injure yourself if you don't use them properly. Free weights require special training, but learning to use them is worth the effort.

Now that I've had training with free weights, here's my basic workout schedule: I spend about 70 percent of my time with weights and 30 percent on cardio exercise (treadmills and ellipticals).

I divide my weight exercises into two-thirds free weights (arm curls, bench presses, leg presses, ab crunches, and chest presses) and one-third weight machines. There's no way to cheat with free weights, so you're sure to get a good workout. But since I still need guidance in doing some exercises safely and properly, I use a combination of free weights and weight machines that fits my experience level.

I cool down on the way home, and I can feel myself getting hungry. I know this is a danger time. It would be easy to grab the first food I see as I walk through the door, but the game's still on, and I don't let myself binge.

Supper varies, but I choose from a short list of options, and I choose foods and serving sizes based on the money I have left to spend. Sometimes we stop on the way home for sub sandwiches. Mine is always turkey, chicken, or roast beef on wheat—with no high-calorie add-ons, only lettuce, onions, peppers, spinach, and other low-cal trimmings. Sometimes I have cereal. I may have another sandwich. My family may have grilled chicken, steak, or salmon, along with steamed vegetables. My grandmother also makes me healthy versions of my favorite foods, like whole-wheat spaghetti with low-fat, low-sodium sauce and ground sirloin meatballs. Whatever I have, I measure serving sizes.

Then I take the stairs to my bedroom two or three at a time. I have a dorm fridge in my room stocked with Coke Zero and bottled water. I drink a Coke Zero and a bottle of water while I do homework and watch TV. I don't have anything else after supper. I had to train myself not to take food to my room, but now it's not even an option.

By the end of a busy day, I've had 2,500 to 2,600 calories. I keep a running tally in my head, and I always round up. If a frozen dinner has 330 calories, I round up to 350. It's easier to keep track, and it gives me a cushion in case I've measured too big a serving. If my weight goes up a pound, I reduce my salary for a week.

PLAYING TO WIN

My approach to fitness is so much like a video game that most kids can catch on quickly to how it's played. In **UFG**, like most games, you travel a maze. You fight the enemy. You progress to a new level. But whatever you do, at every turn you find a choice. And the decision you make takes you on a certain path. Every time I reach a bump in the road and have to make a decision, I try to remember that each decision will take me on a different path.

You start most video games with a certain amount of something vital that you need to complete the game. How you use your resources determines whether you can finish the game. So that's the way I approach each day's eating. I start the day with a certain amount of money/calories. Each time I reach a decision point, I have to decide how much money to spend and whether the foods I buy will be powerful enough to get me through the day. I know I need protein, complex carbs, essential fats, and a variety of vitamins and minerals, and I have to spend my money carefully to be sure I've picked up everything I need by the end of the day. The whole day becomes a strategy.

Sometimes I get hungry. I want a second sandwich or an extra serving of chicken. But I act as my own drill sergeant. I tell myself, "You don't need it. You'll be fine till supper." I control the day with willpower instead of letting my taste buds control it for me. It feels good to be stronger than the foods that call out to me. I haven't had pizza in more than two years.

When someone at school offers me a snack, it's no longer hard to say, "No, thanks." Sure, a gooey snack would taste good for a few minutes, but I never want to go back to those 44-waist jeans.

Sharing the "Secret"

As soon as people started noticing my weight loss, I began to hear, "How did you do it?" They were looking for my secret so they could lose a lot of weight, too.

I understand. I looked for the secret for a long time, so I'm happy to share what I discovered. It's a secret that not many people learn, so when you discover it, I think you have a responsibility to pass it on.

So here's the secret. Write it down. Memorize it. Put it into practice.

The secret is: There is no secret. Weight loss isn't quick. It isn't easy. And gimmicks don't work for long.

Forever weight loss requires three things:

1. **More exercise**
2. **Less food**
3. **Better food choices**

Sorry, but that's the truth. Anyone who tells you it's quick or easy isn't talking about *permanent* weight loss. If the three-step process isn't actually a secret, it *is* well hidden behind hundreds of extreme, temporary "diets." Slow-and-steady weight loss is usually the last resort after every gimmick fails. It takes a long time and a lot of work to get fit, so most of us look for an easy way to do it. But starving, eating nothing but some weird food combination, taking diet pills, and using other gimmicks aren't things you can stick with for the rest of your life. You can lose a little weight for a little while with just about any method, but who wants to go to *all that effort* for something *temporary—and maybe dangerous*? If you want to change from fat to fit forever, you have to eat less, exercise more, and choose your foods carefully.

The idea is simple, but following it is not so easy. I tackle fitness like a major project, and major projects take planning. When I decided to get serious about the ULTIMATE FITNESS GAME (UFG), I knew I needed to set goals. Those goals would be my target.

My granddad is a retired federal agent who now works as a private investigator and serves as a reserve police officer in his town. Since FBI agent is on my short list of career choices, he and I go regularly to the shooting range so he can keep up his skills and I can learn some.

I learn discipline, safety, and precision when we're on the shooting range. But one of the things I've learned is so obvious that it's easy to miss: I learn to focus on a target—to set goals.

When Granddad and I go to the range, we clip on a target, move it back several yards, and take careful aim. Then we pull the target toward us and count the number of holes and where they're placed. Without some way of measuring our accuracy, we'd never know how we were doing or whether we were improving. Each time I get most of my bullets inside the target area, Granddad moves the target back a little farther. I couldn't have started with my target at the back of the range. I started up close, and I'm moving it back a little at a time.

I applied this logic as I set goals for my exercise and weight-loss programs. I knew I had to set some serious goals if I wanted to see serious results, but I couldn't do it all at once. And if I didn't know what I was working for, how would I know if I'd succeeded? So before I counted a calorie or walked on a tread-mill, I set reasonable goals to help me measure my fitness suc-cess. And I incorporated my goals into an overall UFG strategy.

A FITNESS STRATEGY IS PART OF THE "SECRET"

If you want to win a video game, you need a good strategy. If you want to beat a game quickly, you can even download a strategy guide from the Internet. That usually takes the fun out of finding your own way through the mazes and corridors, but if you want to be sure you win, and win quickly, a strategy guide may be the answer.

I knew that UFG would require a good strategy, too. I wanted to move quickly through UFG levels, so I created a strategy guide. Here's my strategy guide for getting fit quickly and stay-ing fit for a lifetime.

I set myself up to win.

I didn't set huge goals, like "I'm going to lose 150 pounds." Goals like that are too big and take too long, and I would have felt defeated before I was out of the starting gate. I started out saying: "I'll lose 20 pounds" and concentrated on reaching that goal. When I lost the first 20 pounds, I set a goal for the next

20. Then the next. That way, I was a winner each time I reached a goal. And since I rarely weighed myself, each time I got on a scale, I had usually surpassed my goal.

I tackled exercise a little at a time.

The first time I faced a treadmill or weight machine, I knew I couldn't expect the maximum workout. I just added one minute or one repetition each time I exercised. I didn't notice the slight increase in effort, but before I knew it, I was getting strong. Check out "The Empty Wheelbarrow" on page 40 for the way I look at this concept.

I changed my eating habits slowly.

When people start a "diet," they usually get all psyched up and want to give it everything they've got. And that's great. But going overboard is a bad idea. In gaming, that's called "overclocking"—running your processor at a faster speed than it's rated. That burns up the processor and can ruin it permanently.

The same thing can happen when people starve themselves. They can only operate on low fuel for a little while. Then they'll decide that getting fit is too hard and give up. I knew if I wanted a program I could stick to—and the energy to stick to the program—I'd have to cut food quantities slowly and include enough food to be healthy. And I knew that, as I increased my exercise level, I'd need more calories just to maintain my weight.

When I first started measuring what I ate, I reduced my intake to 2,000 calories a day. From there, I decreased my

The Empty Wheelbarrow

Imagine that one day you push an empty wheelbarrow around your yard for one minute. You could probably do that, right? Now imagine that the next day, you added one small piece of gravel to the wheelbarrow. If you could push the empty wheelbarrow, can you push it now? Sure. Could you add 10 seconds to your time? Sure.

If you added one piece of gravel to the wheelbarrow every day and pushed the wheelbarrow 10 seconds longer than the day before, the increase would be so slight that you'd never notice the extra load. Now imagine the day when you realize the wheelbarrow is filled to the top with gravel and you're pushing it for an hour—just as easily as you pushed the empty wheelbarrow for one minute.

That's the process you want for effective, *lifestyle* exercise. You're aiming for long-term fitness, so take your time. Naturally, we all want fast results—we're the DSL generation—but why put your effort into something that's so hard you can't continue? Small increases are easier than big ones. Don't overload your bandwidth. Take it slow, one byte at a time. Increase gradually, and before you know it, your actions will be habits, and you'll be living a new and better lifestyle.

intake a little at a time till I was finally eating 1,500 to 1,600 calories a day. But when my exercise increased and I was burning more calories, I upped my calories to 1,800 to 1,900, then to 2,100. Because I was exercising so heavily, I lost weight on 2,100 calories.

Finally, I reached my weight goal. I knew if I continued exercising and eating 2,100 calories a day, I'd keep losing weight. What a great problem with a great solution. To keep from getting *too* thin, I increased my calories to 2,400 to 2,600 a day.

Now, each day when I start a new round of UFG, I base my "money" on my current weight, my weight goal (which is now sometimes *higher* than my current weight), and my exercise plans for the day. Weight adjustments are gradual, a little each day.

I looked for advice and encouragement.

Though I have a fantastic family to encourage me to be healthy and fit, I also find plenty of encouragement and advice on websites and blogs. The Internet puts a global support team at my fingertips, and it's easy to find people of all ages who have lost weight and kept it off.

And it's not hard to find people at school, at church, and in my neighborhood who are trying to get fit. Most of them have some great diet and exercise tips. I've found that if I listen and ask questions, people are usually glad to help me. As far as I'm concerned, there's no such thing as information overload. I take all the advice and tips I can find, sort through them, and keep what works for me. Sometimes the simplest idea will ignite a whole new strategy. Fitness is tough, and there are a lot of us working at it. I love to share what I've learned, and I love to get tips from successful losers. After some tip-sharing, these people become part of my support system, and I become part of theirs.

A SUPPORT TEAM IS PART OF THE "SECRET"

Eventually, exercise became my focus instead of snacking in front of the television. Playing UFC became more important than eating whatever, whenever. When I analyzed how the change occurred, I knew I hadn't done it alone. If someone had asked me what resources I used to get fit, I would have followed all the Oscar winners and said, "I'd like to thank the *Academy*."

But my thanks go to Chrysalis Experiential *Academy*, as well as to the U.S. Marine Corps, Microsoft Zune, the YMCA, Coke Zero, and all my family members, friends, fitness trainers, and others who continue to support me. Everybody needs workout partners and encouragers, and these are mine.

Friends and Heroes

Five months into my exercise program, I changed schools. My new school, Chrysalis Experiential Academy, was filled with opportunity and challenge. The school's name is perfect because it's a chrysalis where caterpillars can become butterflies, a place where kids reach their potential. I loved it from the first day. Richard, the school's director, is fantastic. He soon became my mentor and friend.

Great school director. Fantastic teachers. Cool kids. The perfect support team for reaching my fitness goal. Naturally, I wanted to make a good impression, so when some of the guys took a camping trip that first fall, I decided to go, even though camping wasn't as comfortable for me as working with my computer. I was feeling strong, but the weight was coming off slowly and only those closest to me could see how hard I'd worked and what progress I'd made. When I entered Chrysalis, I was still a big guy.

Not long into the camping trip, the group decided to take a canoe ride, so we lined up to rent life jackets. The park had no life jacket that would fit me. I convinced everyone that I was a good enough swimmer that I didn't need a life jacket

But once I passed the embarrassing life jacket hurdle, I still had the canoe ride ahead of me. A couple of guys got into a canoe and called to me to join them. When I started in, the canoe tipped drastically. The kids were great, and no one said anything.

Chrysalis was just the school I needed to help me set goals and be persistent in reaching them. The school's healthy, positive discipline carried over to my workout and eating programs. I could feel myself becoming more disciplined in every area.

Family

In addition to my newfound school support, my family remained constant in their encouragement. Since I was too young to have a driver's license, my commitment to exercise became my family's commitment. No matter how tired Mom was after a long day, we went to the Y. And the few times she couldn't go, my grandmother drove me.

The U.S. Marines

Once I got to the Y, I depended on a couple of resources to get me through day after day of workouts. Most of the Y's treadmills and elliptical equipment had TVs with closed captions, but I needed my fast-paced Marine Corps cadences. So I wore my Zune and ear buds every time I worked out.

Experts

Dyan, my trainer at the Y, eventually took another job, but she still met with me occasionally, just as a friend. She was proud of the progress I'd made under her guidance, and her approval meant a lot to me. Her expert advice and her one-on-one guidance made a huge difference as I played **UFG**.

I also found plenty of advice on Internet blogs and websites, but I soon learned that I had to examine all the advice carefully. All sorts of people are more than happy to offer advice, and some isn't safe or healthy. I learned to stick with reliable websites like www.WebMD.com, www.cdc.gov, www.health vault.com, and www.ahealthyme.com. There I found free advice from real experts. I still check out these sites to stay informed on nutrition and exercise news.

Rewards

Drinking Coke Zero kept me from feeling deprived, so I'm including it as one of my supporters. Before fitness became important to me, I could consume 500 to 800 calories a day in regular soft drinks. Switching to Coke Zero helped me lose weight because it's calorie-free. My weakness is wanting a Coke, and with Coke Zero, I feel like I can still have one. Real Coke taste, zero calories. I'm Zero's biggest promoter!

People sometimes remind me that diet drinks have artificial sweeteners. I remind them that most kids drink some sort of soft drinks, and drinks loaded with sugar put kids in danger of diabetes, heart disease, and other obesity-related diseases. I usually have a bottle of water with my Coke Zero, and I think the diluted Zero is healthier for me than a sugary drink.

Besides, every negative behavior has to be replaced with a positive one. Without Coke Zero, I'd have a hole in my routine that kept nagging to be filled. I replaced my craving for flavored milk drinks and regular soft drinks with Coke Zero, and I'm satisfied. (My goofy brother says he can eat roasted almonds with his eyes shut and imagine they're a chocolate bar with almonds, but with the chocolate licked off. Hey, whatever works for you.)

Fans

If you're looking for a support system, you can grow your own by just starting the fitness process. When I first began my exercise program, only my trainer, Dyan, noticed a difference. But soon other Y members noticed.

"Are you that kid who used to wear sunglasses, jeans, and boots?" they'd ask. When I told them yes, they'd shake their heads in amazement. They'd congratulate me. Two people said, "I don't notice many people here, but I notice you."

I started making friends at the Y. When I first started working out, I sent out the message to leave me alone. I was angry because I had such a long road ahead. I watched people run for a half hour and knew I could only walk at 3 mph. But I tackled one small goal at a time, and eventually I had a lot in common with the others at the Y.

People at school noticed my weight loss, too. Our assistant

director asked how I'd lost the weight. Kids asked for workout advice. The compliments encouraged me. The people who bothered to say "wow" have become a special group of supporters, and it's a group anyone can gather, regardless of how much support they have from family and friends.

Enemy-Turned-Friend

Believe it or not, the scale became a supporter instead of a monster I hid from. The winter after I started at my new school, I picked up a nasty cold. This time, I didn't try to talk Mom out of taking me to Dr. Bagheri's. The last time I visited his office, I'd weighed more than 250 pounds. This time, the nurse set the scale at 150 and started moving the balance bar. I started to tell her to add another weight. Before I could speak, she balanced the scale at 194.

The next spring, I weighed myself at the mall, with my heavy running shoes on. I was down to 182—I'd lost 100 pounds since starting my workouts at the Y, and I was 115 below my highest weight. About that time, I applied for my driver's permit and was able to give my weight as 180.

I didn't let myself focus on weight, and it was August before I weighed myself again, this time on a balance scale at my grandparents' house. I took off my belt buckle, cell phone, and shoes. As I slid the bar to a perfect balance, I knew my efforts were worth it. Every grunt, every sweaty day at the Y, every rejected cookie couldn't compare with the number on my grandparents' scale: 160. I've maintained that weight—actually 10 to 15 pounds under—since that day.

Once I had vivid dreams of weighing 180. It was the lowest

weight I could imagine. Now if the scale registered 180, I'd freak. I'd be 35 pounds above my normal weight.

My supportive school, friends, and family. My Zune with Marine Corps cadences. A supportive and well-equipped place to work out. And a zero-calorie treat at the end of a workout. These are the "members" of my personal UFG support team.

A lot of people have told me they were impressed that I got healthy all on my own, but that's not true. I figured out a system that worked for me, and I figured out what and who I needed to make the system succeed.

I'm fortunate to have a family and school that support me. But anyone can find support if they look for it. If no one else had ever told me, "You can do it," I would have heard it from my Marine Corps cadences.

What's *your* ideal support system? Consider your tastes, lifestyle, and circumstances as you create a customized network that gives you just the help you need to get fit and stay that way.

DOING YOUR HOMEWORK IS PART OF THE "SECRET"

I didn't want to go on a crash diet. I wanted to plan a strategy for UFG that would let me lose weight once, for a lifetime. For something so important, I knew I needed to take my time.

I had a couple of false starts before I got serious about fitness, and I think the reason I wasn't successful was that I jumped in too fast, without knowing how to go about it. I was so sick of being overweight that I wanted to lose pounds quickly. I didn't want to take time to figure out what needed to be done and how to do it.

When I have a school assignment, I first listen to the teacher's instructions. I figure out what's required of me, and then I create a plan to accomplish it. As much as I want to get the assignment out of the way, I have to know what the assignment is if I'm going to complete it successfully. If, on Monday morning, my teacher gives the class a warning, "You'll need to turn in a report by Friday," and I leave the room immediately and start work, I could end up doing a lot of work for nothing. If I don't wait to get all the facts, I might do my report on the wrong subject. I might type a report when the teacher's expecting an oral report or even a videotaped one. Clarification on the front end can save a lot of trouble later on.

It's the same with fitness. When I slowed down and did my homework, the whole process became easier. When I really got down to business and started taking my fitness program seriously, I asked myself the following questions:

What's my ideal weight, and how far am I from reaching it?

Once I got serious, I didn't just make up a "dream weight" figure. I checked out online weight charts and found the weight that's healthiest for my height, age, and body structure. At one time, my dream was to weigh 180. I know now that 180 is a little too much for my frame. Once I realized that I was capable of losing the weight, I didn't want to settle for anything but total fitness.

It was important for me to know how much weight I had to lose, but I didn't make that overwhelming total my goal.

Instead, I set small goals of 20 pounds at a time. (See "Twenty Pounds at a Time" below.)

Twenty Pounds at a Time

Even though you'll break your overall weight-loss goal into smaller segments, you need to know your ideal weight when you begin your fitness program. Subtract your ideal weight from your current weight and divide that amount into 20-pound increments. Each time you lose 20 pounds, you can celebrate that loss—but not with a Twinkie. And you can also calculate the percentage you've achieved of your overall weight-loss goal. For instance, if you have 140 pounds to lose, you'll have seven 20-pound segments. When you lose your first 20 pounds, you'll be one-seventh of the way to your ultimate goal. That sounds lots better than thinking you have 120 pounds more to lose.

Overall, though, I'd recommend taking the focus off weight as much as possible. Staying away from the scale helps you think of your fitness program as a new way of life instead of a diet. It was easier for me not to focus on weight at all, at least until I got near my goal. And each time I weighed, I had the advantage of seeing a big change. If I'd had access to a good scale on a regular basis, I probably would have weighed myself more often, but I hope no more than once a month. Now that I've reached my ideal weight, I weigh several times a week because I want to catch a slight weight gain before it gets out of control. So my strategy is "weigh seldom while you're losing and often when you've lost."

Why am I overweight?

I knew I was overweight because I wasn't getting enough exercise, I was overeating, and I was eating the wrong foods. And maybe I *had* inherited the fat gene, but it didn't have to rule my life. The choice was mine, and I chose to be thin. Check out "Heredity or Family Food Choices?" on page 51 for more on this.

When do I overeat?

What time of day do I eat the most? What are the circumstances when I overeat? Evening homework and TV time used to be a big calorie challenge for me. And the bad thing was that I hardly got to enjoy the food. I ate mindlessly while concentrating on my computer or a TV show. Now, when I feel hungry while watching TV, I keep my hands busy. Dumbbells are good, and so are the adjustable hand grips that athletes use to strengthen their grip. I got mine at a sporting goods store, but they're also available at discount stores and online.

After school was another time when I was tempted to overeat, probably because of bad food choices earlier in the day. For more on this, check out "Lunchtime's Arch Enemies" on page 52.

How do I overeat?

Do I eat more when I'm alone or with friends? Do I enjoy the taste of my food, or do I eat mindlessly? Once I answered these questions and knew my danger zones, I set out to combat them. I realized that I tended to eat more when I was alone, so now I do my best to avoid long, lazy afternoons in my room. I get

Heredity or Family Food Choices?

Is your whole family obese? If so, then heredity may play a part in your size. Of course, your whole family may have the same bad eating habits. Think about your family—grandparents, parents, aunts, uncles, sisters, brothers, and cousins. If everyone in your family seems to struggle with weight, you may have to rewrite some codes, but you can lose weight. Knowing what you're up against helps you know how to tackle the problem.

If just your immediate family is overweight, maybe the main culprit is family food choices. That can be just about as tough as heredity because you have to eat what's set before you or come up with alternate meals.

If you're the only one in your family who's large, what makes you different? Maybe you've had some unusual stress. If so, you can train yourself to fight stress with exercise.

It's worth taking the time to figure out where your weight problem's coming from. When I get a new video game, one of the first things I want to know is, "Who's the opponent? Who or what am I trying to conquer?" It's that way with UFG, too. Once you know the factors that contribute to your extra weight, you'll have an idea of what you're up against, and you'll advance to a new UFG level. The "why" is one opponent you have to combat. Check out the rest of this section for other UFG opponents.

Lunchtime's Arch Enemies

Schools often have to space out lunch hours, and in some schools, kids have lunch as early as 10:30 AM and as late as 2:00 PM.

If lunch is early and you have a long bus ride home, by the time you reach your kitchen you may be in the eat-whatever mode, grabbing cookies, chips, and snack cakes. If that's the case, try to have some fast, healthy snacks available. I'm not a big fruit eater, so I try to keep whole-grain crackers (I know exactly how many calories are in a serving and how many crackers equal a serving) and fresh veggies on hand.

If lunch is late, you may find yourself eating everyone else's leftovers, buying or bringing extra carbs, and doing an all-around tank-up to make up for a deprived morning. The key here may be using more of your daily calories for a substantial breakfast with lots of protein. It's the end-of-the-day total calories that count, so think: big breakfast equals sane lunch.

out and do something. I walk around my neighborhood. I go to the mall. As a last resort, I even hang out with my kid brother.

I usually don't eat as much when I'm with friends, unless our activities revolve around food, like eating in a restaurant or going to the movies. When an activity has a food-focus, I use self-coaching (more about that in Chapter 10). I tell myself, *The choice you make will affect the rest of your day and even your lifetime.*

With that reminder front and center, I can go to a movie and choose a diet drink instead of a free-refills monster bucket of popcorn and a large regular drink. I've learned that if I can get past the ordering process, it isn't so bad living with my decision. I concentrate on the company of friends, a good movie, and the taste of my diet drink. I give these things my full attention, and after just a few minutes I notice that my friends have eaten their high-calorie snacks and everyone has settled down to watch the movie. I feel powerful that I got through the snack time without ruining my **UFG** score.

What foods tempt me most?

Most overweight people have a certain type of food that's their downfall. For me, it was carbs in the form of starches. I loved them plain, and I loved them covered with more carbs. Grits, biscuits, and many Southern recipes are starches, pure and simple. Cookies, breakfast rolls, and snack cakes are starches in disguise—carb starch coated with carb sugar—carbs on carbs. Once I realized how much of my diet was carbs, they lost a lot of their appeal.

Some people crave carb starches (potatoes, bread, crackers, chips, corn) or carb sugar (soft drinks, candy, rich desserts). Some love fat, as in bacon, fried foods, and heavy sauces. The key is to identify the pest and exterminate it.

Where do I stand on the three steps to fitness?

Do I eat the right foods? Do I eat the right portions? How much do I exercise? Most people who struggle with their weight have problems with at least two of these steps. I had problems with all three. But that was okay. Once I knew my weak areas, I could determine my game plan and know what type of goals to set.

SETTING GOALS IS PART OF THE "SECRET"

Goals are great ways to measure success, in life and in UFC. But the key to successful goals is setting the right ones and making them achievable.

Setting the wrong goal is like running toward the wrong goalpost in a football game. You might run hard and fast, but you won't be pleased with the results. If your goal is just to lose weight any way you can, you may work hard to achieve that goal, but the results may be short-term and you'll be setting the same goal this time next year.

Setting a goal that can't be achieved will put you on a road to failure before you start. You may think, *My goal is to lose ten pounds a week*. That's a wish, not a goal, and you'd be doomed to fail. If you set a goal of two pounds a week, each week's success will give you confidence for the next week.

I set the right goals.

If I aim at the wrong target, it's no big deal if I hit it. So I always make sure my goal is worthy of the effort I'm putting into my fitness program. To be worthy, it has to be a lifetime goal. I don't waste my time on short-term fitness and weight loss that I won't or can't continue. I don't want to look back a year from now and say, "Wow, I starved myself for a month, lost twenty pounds and then gained it all back. What a waste."

How much better to say, "It took me four months to lose twenty pounds, but I lost another twenty pounds the next four months, and another the next four. Now, a year later, I weigh sixty pounds less than when I started playing UFG."

I broke down goals into bite-size pieces.

My overall goals were to lose weight and have a strong, healthy body. I broke those big goals into lots of smaller ones. I would lose twenty pounds. I would reduce my sodium, fat, and carb consumption by 10 percent. I would do these things by decreasing my calories, increasing my exercise, and making better food choices.

CALCULATIONS ARE PART OF THE "SECRET"

I'm constantly calculating calories because consuming too many made me supersized and not consuming enough could make me too weak to work out. So to ensure a good balance, I also calculate the calories I burn while exercising.

I've learned that my BMR (the calories I'd burn if I did absolutely *nothing* all day) is 1,850. I know I burn 350 calories for forty-five minutes of free weights and 625 calories for five miles at 6 mph on the treadmill. And I know that how hard I work out is at least as important as how long. If I use heavier dumbbells for my arm curls or go faster on the elliptical, I can increase the calories I burn without spending more time at the gym.

When I've calculated the calories I'll burn for the day, I add this number to my BMR. Then I add 10 percent for the calories I'll use to digest my food. If I want to lose weight, I eat fewer calories than I'll burn. If I want to maintain my weight, I try to eat about the same number of calories I'll burn.

Here are the daily calculations I use to keep score in **UFG**:

- ↪ I create a new formula each morning: BMR calories + exercise calories + an additional 10 percent of calories for digestion = my maximum calories for the day.
- ↪ I count every calorie I take in and round up if I'm unsure.
- ↪ I factor in my need for vitamins, minerals, and other nutrients.
- ↪ I factor in the calories burned during exercise.
- ↪ I subtract from my menus as many calories as possible that come from sugar carbs and their evil cousins, saturated fats, trans fats, and cholesterol.
- ↪ I subtract from my menus the unnecessary calories in condiments, sauces, and other trimmings.
- ↪ Throughout the day, I calculate my UFG progress. I subtract the calories I consume from the calories I need for the day (my formula). If the numbers are about equal, I'll maintain my weight. If I've eaten more calories than I burned, I'll gain weight. If I've burned more calories than I ate, I'll lose weight.

It takes 3,500 calories more than we need to gain a pound and 3,500 less than we need to lose a pound. If we consume 500 calories more than we need each day, we'll gain a pound a week. If we consume 500 calories less than we need each day, we'll lose a pound a week.

It may sound complicated, but most of us play more difficult video games every day. I just consider calorie counting the way I keep score in **UFG**. And my prize is a pair of 30-waist jeans.

BEING AWARE IS PART OF THE "SECRET"

Making better food choices meant understanding what nutrients I needed and in what quantities, what vitamins and minerals each food contained per serving, and what a serving size really looked like. It wasn't too complicated once I understood the basics. I soon learned that once I ate all the foods I needed to be healthy and to have energy for working out, I didn't have calories left to waste on junk foods. In UFG, every food had to move me toward my end-of-the-day goal of balancing my calorie intake with the healthy calories my body needed for that day. To keep moving toward my goal, I had to be aware of everything I put into my mouth. I couldn't allow myself a bite, a taste, or a nibble of anything without "buying" it with my UFG money.

I used the Internet to keep myself aware of everything I needed for fitness and why I needed it. I charted my diet and exercise on a weight-loss website. I used search engines to find BMI and BMR calculators. I read the health Q&A section of fitness websites. I researched target heart rates. I spent a lot of time on www.acaloriecounter.com and other calorie-calculating sites.

Sometimes I watched the television program *The Biggest Loser*. I remember an episode when one of the medical advisers put a model of a heart into 100 pounds of pig fat. He told viewers, "This is what your heart has to support when you're overweight. This is how difficult it will be to find your heart if you have surgery, which you may very well need if you stay obese." Talk about being aware! That demonstration scared me into facing reality, and I wanted to improve my health. But the journey from fat to fit seemed overwhelming. I had to break the journey into short distances for it to be manageable.

MARKING MILESTONES IS PART OF THE "SECRET"

I learned to use small successes to help me move forward in UFG. Marking each milestone gave me the incentive to keep charging toward my ultimate goal of total fitness. When that goal seemed far away, I'd remember how far I'd come.

I used to see pictures in my mom's magazines of people who had lost 100 pounds. Instead of encouraging me, the pictures discouraged me. I thought, *Wow, if it's so hard to lose 100 pounds that they write about you in a magazine, what are the odds of me doing it?* But when I started noticing small changes of my own, those people in the magazines became my encouragers. I started thinking, *They did it, and so can I.*

Marking my own successes changed my reaction to the success stories I saw in magazines. When I bought new jeans with a smaller waist or ran a mile on the treadmill without stopping, I began thinking of myself as a winner. I knew I would someday be one of the success stories.

I remember a particular day when I knew I was going to win UFG. I saw a pair of my brother Elliott's jeans lying on the bed, a size-38 waist. I had always considered Elliott skinny because he was smaller than me, and though he loved to wear his jeans baggy, I would still consider it a major coup if I could squeeze into them. I decided to try on his jeans when no one was around.

When I fastened those size-38 jeans and realized they were too big, I knew I was going to make it. It was then that I realized, "Oh, wow. If I can do this much, I can keep it up."

Another milestone was when I ran a 10-minute mile. My lungs were on fire, but I'd done it. I'd run a mile. I didn't care about the pain. Just seeing the treadmill click over to one mile was like a shot of adrenaline. I'd run 6 mph for 10 minutes. I can't tell you how powerful that realization made me feel. It may have been a small milestone in the overall UFG, but to me it was a giant step forward.

DOING THE NUMBERS IS PART OF THE "SECRET"

From the start, an essential part of getting fit with UFG was doing the numbers. If I didn't add up everything I put into my mouth, I knew I'd put in more than I intended. And if I didn't keep a record of my exercise, I wouldn't be challenged to sweat a little more at each workout. I had to be calculating.

Keep Up with Progress

The YMCA where I work out keeps an electronic record of the exercises I do. I punch my member code into each machine and complete the program my personal trainer assigned. When I punch out, I get a total number of pounds lifted and miles run. I can also chart my progress online. But you don't need an elaborate record-keeping system to chart your progress. Keep track of your exercise in a notebook or on your computer, but keep track. Having a visual record of your exercise keeps you wanting to increase your program. And watching the numbers go up makes you feel like a winner.

Keep Track of Calories

Tracking calories actually helps me resist the foods I shouldn't have. The more I concentrate on playing UFG, the less time I have to think about the foods that tempt me. And the closer I keep track, the clearer I see that I can't have half a pizza and still have enough calories for all the healthy foods I need.

I know I've said it before, but it's important enough to mention again: The only way to keep an accurate calorie count is to know what a serving size looks like. You have to quantify everything, or it's too easy to cheat. Measure a real serving of anything and you may discover you've been having three times the calories you thought you were having. I like foods packaged in individual serving sizes because there's no guesswork. They cost more per serving, but I probably pay less overall because I eat less.

Stick to a Budget

As I plan each day's calorie budget, I know I can "buy" any food I really want. If a small serving of rich dessert is 300 calories and I have 2,500 calories allotted for the day, I can have the dessert. But I can have a lean turkey sandwich on no-sugar whole-wheat bread for fewer calories than the dessert. The sandwich provides more energy, and even though the dessert makes me feel full right away, the sandwich stays with me longer and helps me eat less in the long run. It's all a matter of making the right choices and using my calorie budget wisely.

I soon learned that eating is like shopping at a store with no returns. Once I eat something, I have to live with my decision all day. When I'm out of calories, I can't buy any more food. The more I focus on spending my calories, the more it becomes a game, and the more carefully I protect my stash of calories.

Each day's a fresh start, and I rarely carry over calories to the next day, not even on holidays. It gets too complicated and too easy to cheat. Anyway, it doesn't seem worth it to blow hundreds of calories on a holiday dessert. I'd rather have baked chicken, steamed vegetables, and fresh-baked whole-grain bread. If I really want a cookie, I break one, eat half, and calculate it into my calories for the day. But that's feeding the dinosaur that I'm trying hard to make extinct, so I try not to do that too often. My family has created low-calorie versions of some healthier desserts, like pumpkin pie, that give us the taste and the nutrients without feeding our cravings (visit www.cutting myselfinhalf.com for this and other recipes). Now that I'm down to my ideal weight, I can afford a piece of healthy no-crust pumpkin pie, full of vitamin A and less than 100 calories.

KNOWING THE GOOD STUFF IS PART OF THE "SECRET"

Eating right is not just a matter of counting calories. Making sure I get all the nutrients I need is like a sublevel of UFG calculations. I know my body needs carbs, fat, and protein to be healthy, along with all of the necessary vitamins and minerals. You need these nutrients, too, but there are some things you should know about them:

About Carbs

Carbs controlled me for so long that I'm determined to control them. Even now, I try to stay under 90 percent of the carbs allowed for a day. But carbs aren't all bad. They're actually necessary for a healthy and fit body. They provide lots of vitamins and minerals, as well as fiber. You just have to choose them carefully and make sure to keep them at or under the recommended percentage of your diet.

Carbs come in three types: sugar, starch, and fiber. My maximum for sugar carbs is 125 grams a day. Sugar's in practically everything, even canned vegetables, so it adds up fast. We need some sugar, but getting enough is rarely a problem in North America.

Fruits have lots of natural sugar but also lots of important nutrients. Even milk has sugar calories, along with lots of vitamins and minerals. But most of the sugar we eat is just quick hollow energy with very few strength-building nutrients. Soft drinks, candy, cakes, and pies are mostly sugar. For the most part, sugar is a lousy way to get carbs.

Starch is the way to go when you're spending your carb calories. Foods made from plants are the best source of starch: corn, potatoes, beans, bananas, bread (whole grain is best), rice (choose brown if you have a choice), cereal (whole grain), and pasta (whole wheat if possible). These carbs also provide vitamins and minerals. The problem with starches is that we like them covered with fat. If we can keep from covering our healthy carbs with butter, gravy, and creamy sauces, they're healthy foods.

Fiber's good, and we need it for healthy bodies. But fiber's like eating a tree branch. It may have some vitamins and minerals, but it has no calories because our bodies can't digest it. So fiber is sort of free carbs. The best ways to get fiber are eating brown rice and whole-grain breads and pasta and eating the edible skins of vegetables and fruits. If you've been eating white bread and rice and peeling your fruits and veggies, your taste buds will have to do some adjusting. But once you get used to the new tastes, you'll find that these natural foods are more filling and actually taste better. It just takes awhile to retrain your taste buds.

Carbs are also divided into simple and complex. Simple carbs are high sugar and are found in candy, soft drinks, and snack cakes. They go through your body fast, and they give you a burst of quick energy. But they leave you hungry soon after eating them, and they have very few nutrients.

Complex carbs are usually attached to fiber, and they take longer to go through your body. They give you a full feeling longer. They're found mainly in whole grains and vegetables, and they're loaded with vitamins and minerals.

So bottom line, carbs are as good as the ones you choose. Do your research to learn more.

About Protein

Protein is the key to building new cells and muscles and repairing damaged ones. We need it to grow, repair, and maintain our bodies. I try to take in at least 70 grams of protein a day and up to 120 if I can. Most people need 50–60 grams, but I use extra protein for workout energy. Lean beef, fish, seafood, white-meat poultry, egg whites, pork tenderloin, beans, and no-fat or low-fat dairy products are good choices for protein. And to be sure I get enough protein, each day I have an energy bar with 28–32 grams of protein. You'll need to find out how much protein is ideal for you.

About Fat

We need fat to store vitamins A and D, and for other things, too. It's necessary but definitely not something you want in large quantities or something you have to go looking for. Most of us get plenty of fat without trying, but we get the wrong kinds. We need "good fat"—omega 3—for a healthy heart and lower cholesterol, but we only need it in small amounts.

Each gram of fat has 9 calories, and a gram of carbs or protein has only 4 calories. Too much fat increases the risk of cancer, high blood pressure, stroke, and heart disease. It's good to limit our diets to no more than 30 percent fat calories. I maintain a low-fat diet, usually under 15 grams per meal.

Fats come in three forms: saturated fats, unsaturated fats, and trans fats. If you're talking calories, they're the same. If you're talking healthy arteries, stay away from saturated and trans fats. Try to find products that say "zero trans fats."

Fat is a big part of packaged snacks and pastries, and these foods also contain hollow sugar calories. There's no room for them in a healthy diet. We can reduce the fat in our diets even more by using fat-free milk and cheese and forgetting butter or margarine on our bread. And the most obvious way to cut down on fat is to cut the fat from meat, take the skin off chicken, and drain fried and even baked meat on paper towels. Again, do your research to make sure the fat you eat is the healthy kind.

About Micronutrients

Macronutrients—proteins, carbs, and fats—are what we think most about when we start getting fit, but they're not the whole nutrition story. Micronutrients are also must-haves for a healthy body. They're usually found in small amounts in the foods we eat, and that's okay because our bodies only need them in small amounts. They include vitamins and minerals like calcium and iron, and things we don't think much about, like copper, fluorine, and zinc. But micronutrients are like the little stitches in the seat of your pants. You probably don't notice them until they're missing.

For instance, copper helps give our skin and hair their color. Fluorine and zinc help fight tooth decay. So see what I mean? Without small amounts of these micronutrients, we'd soon look and feel a little worse.

We don't want to overdose on these bite-size nutrients, but we definitely need our daily micro-dose. We can usually find the micronutrients we need in a healthy diet, but it's good to do your homework to be sure your diet is giving you the micronutrients you need. If you're unsure, a vitamin/mineral supplement is a good way to keep each "stitch" in place.

I've talked a lot about nutrients, but remember that I'm not a nutrition expert. I'm a kid who's done his best to figure out what I need to stay fit and healthy. Don't take my word as the latest and best. I search my favorite websites regularly to learn as much as I can about nutrition, and I suggest you do that, too. You'll find basic information and new health updates if you visit these sites regularly: www.WebMD.com, www.cdc.gov, www.healthvault.com, and www.ahealthyme.com.

READING LABELS IS PART OF THE "SECRET"

Reading labels helps me control my intake of potentially dangerous food additives and also to make sure I'm getting enough of the nutrients my body needs. At first, reading labels seemed like a big deal, but after a while, I started doing it automatically. Now, when someone says, "Have you tried these new cheesy chips?" I pick up the bag and read the claims on the front. If it says "baked, not fried," "zero trans fat," and "multigrain," I consider trying a couple. I flip over to the back and read the nutrition facts. The label on a healthy chip may look something like this:

Nutrition Facts

Serving Size 1 ounce
Servings Per Container 7

Amount Per Serving

Calories 140	**Calories from Fat 50**

	% Daily Value
Total Fat 6g	9%
Saturated Fat 1g	4%
Trans Fat 0g	
Cholestrol 0mg	
Sodium 160mg	7%
Potassium 70mg	2%
Total Carbs 19mg	6%
Dietary Fiber 2g	2%
Sugars 2g	
Protein 2g	2%

Vitamin A 0g	
Vitamin C 0g	
Calcium 0g	
Iron 2%	
Vitamin E 8g	
Thiamin 2%	
Riboflavin 2%	
Niacin 2%	
Vitamin B6 4%	
Phosphorus 6%	
Magnesium 4%	
Zinc 2%	

It doesn't take a math genius to figure I'd have to eat fifty servings of chips at 7,000 calories to get all the protein I needed for the day, so these chips won't contribute much to the energy I need for exercise. Ditto for their contribution to micronutrients. The only thing the chips are good for is carbs and calories, but they could be worse. They could be fried with saturated fats. They're not a bad choice if you have calories to spare, but they're not as great as the little heart symbol on the front of the package pretends. So when someone offers me chips like these, in less than a minute, I've scanned the bag and decided if I want to spend my calories on them.

When someone hands me an unfamiliar snack, it's sort of like taking a high-level UFG challenge. When I can make a quick decision because I understand what macronutrients and micronutrients I need, I'm glad I've done my homework.

BUILDING MUSCLE IS PART OF THE "SECRET"

Advancing in UFG takes more than just losing weight. Not only do I want to be thin; I also want to be strong and healthy. I love the feel of toned muscles, and as soon as I understood how muscles rebuild and how to turn fat into muscle, I was on my way to a toned body.

Some people who lose weight end up with skin that wiggles and hangs from their bones. After working so hard to get rid of the bodies they tried to hide, all they do is exchange them for other bodies they want to keep under wraps.

I wanted to lose weight slowly, and I wanted to replace my fat with muscle. Dyan, my trainer, explained how muscles grow. I found it so fascinating that I did more research on the Internet.

Muscles don't grow just by expanding. They actually rip, or tear, and then rebuild by scarring, a microlayer at a time. The first step is to rip the muscles, and the best way to do that is by lifting weights and straining the muscles through intense exercise. As you rip muscle tissue, you release endorphins (natural pain- and stress-fighting chemicals). That's what gives you a "runner's high," a feeling of exhilaration.

Once muscles are ripped, sleep is critical to rebuild them.

Muscles rebuild just like a scab covers a cut and makes a thin scar. Next time you lift weights, your muscles will rip again, then rebuild again at night. Each layer is thinner than a sheet of paper and toned muscles are layers of scars. When you start to see your muscles bulk up, you know you've been going to the gym faithfully and for a long time. You have the "scars" to prove it.

Now that I've shared my "secrets," I'll bet you'll agree that they're not secrets at all. They're just practical ideas for taking fitness seriously and putting as much effort into UFG as you'd put into anything that's important to you, like a hobby or sport, a new video game, or a major school project.

There are no secrets or tricks to a lifetime of fitness. Gimmicks and shortcuts are tempting when you're starting down a long road to fitness, but if you want to reach the finish line and celebrate for the rest of your life, remember: Weight loss isn't quick. It isn't easy. And forever weight loss requires three things:

1. **More exercise**
2. **Less food**
3. **Better food choices**

5

Overcoming Obstacles

Tell your parents that you're stressed, and they may tell you that you have no idea what stress is and just wait till you're an adult and have to earn a living and raise a family and—well, you can imagine the rest. But kids have their own kinds of stress, and, depending on how we handle it, our stress can be just as harmful as an adult's.

Here's a quick quiz to see if you recognize "kid stress":

→ Do you ever wish you weren't the last kid chosen for a baseball team?

→ Do you wish your grades were as good as the other kids' grades?

→ Do your friends pressure you to do things you know you shouldn't?

→ Are you ever tempted to do things you know are wrong, just because others are doing them?

→ Have you been bullied by other kids?

→ Have you been the punch line of other kids' jokes?

→ Do you sometimes wonder how you'll have time to do your homework, finish your chores, and take your trombone (or

other) lesson? In other words, do you ever feel overbooked?
→ Does a major test put you in panic mode?
→ Has your best friend ever hurt your feelings?
→ When you try to talk to someone you have a crush on, do you freeze?
→ Do you have trouble getting along with your brother or sister?
→ Do you sometimes feel that your parents aren't listening when you have a problem? Or do you feel like they're too involved and won't let you make decisions you're capable of making?

Every yes is a stress.

Kids have stress, and we all find ways to deal with it, kind of like battling obstacles in a video game. But many ways of dealing with stress, like battle strategies, are self-destructive. Sometimes kids smoke, drink, or use drugs. Sometimes they turn inward and get depressed. And sometimes they turn to comfort foods. Besides harming us physically, these things don't get rid of stress. They just bury it, and sooner or later it will resurface.

I never thought my overeating was a reaction to stress, but after playing the ULTIMATE FITNESS GAME (UFG) for a while, I know now that it was. I'd been a chubby child, but my weight skyrocketed after some major changes in my life all occurred within two and a half years, when I was ten, eleven, and twelve. Here are the things that caused my major stress. Maybe you'll relate to some of them.

MY MAJOR STRESSORS

When I was ten, my great-aunt Ann was murdered. Aunt Ann shared Christmases with us and was as close to Elliott and me as a grandmother. The whole family went through a terrible time as we dealt with losing her. It was almost five years before the killer was convicted of robbery and murder, and during that time, lots of family dinner conversations centered on the investigation. My family was careful not to discuss details of the murder when Elliott and I were around, but we knew it was violent—it was even featured on *America's Most Wanted*. I had trouble understanding how someone could kill such a kind person, and though I was probably too young to totally comprehend how terrible the situation was, I saw what it was doing to the rest of the family and that created stress for me.

Two years later, in the early morning, while we were still groggy and confused, our house caught fire. I'd seen fires on TV, of course, but that was nothing compared to seeing my whole street lined with fire trucks, all rushing to my house. Most of our upstairs was ruined either by fire or the water used to put out the fire. Because the fire had begun smoldering while we slept, it took a long time for Elliott and me to feel safe going to sleep at night. I became worried about our family dying in a fire, and I asked for a fire extinguisher for my room. I still have one.

I can still remember how I felt the morning of the fire as I stood outside in my underwear, watching our house burn. My heart was pounding, my knees were wobbling, my teeth were chattering, and I was stuttering from the stress and the cold.

Then, a few months later, my mother got a divorce. It was

the best thing for our family, and I was proud of her for getting out of a bad situation, but we were now a single-parent family.

And finally, a new principal took over the middle school my brother and I attended. Any student who didn't fit his strict mold was constantly in trouble, and Elliott and I weren't cookie-cutter kids. We dreaded going to school each day, and by Christmas, our family had decided to change schools. The next year, my brother and I attended awesome schools, but the stress from the first school left emotional scars.

It was during these years of unusual stress that I went from chubby kid to obese teen. I ate mindlessly until I could eat no more. I called it "whatever, I-don't-care" eating, but I know now that I was eating to deal with my stress.

Once I started eating to combat stress, it was hard to stop. And the higher my weight climbed, the more out of reach fitness became. But fast forward two years. When I finally decided to take control of my health, my life, my fitness, and my future, I learned that my fitness plan had a built-in super stress buster.

THE BEST STRESS BUSTER

After five or six months on my exercise routine—about the length of time it takes for a new behavior to become a habit—I realized that when I was angry or stressed or frustrated, I no longer grabbed a box of snack cakes. Instead, I begged Mom to take me to the Y. I could feel the tenseness leave my body as I ran at full speed four, five, and six miles, listening to Marine

Corps cadences on my Zune. It wasn't until I realized how much I craved exercise during stressful times (and how perfectly the treadmill replaced honey buns) that I knew my eating was stress-driven.

Not all of my stress was major like murder, fire, and divorce. Some was typical teen stuff. For instance, sometimes I waited till the last minute to do homework. Or Elliott and I would pick at each other like most brothers do. Or friends hurt my feelings. Or teachers blamed me for things I didn't do. Teen stuff, but genuine stress. I knew everyday stress wasn't going to just go away, but now I had a healthy outlet for it.

THE ULTIMATE TEST FOR MY NEW STRESS BUSTER

Exercise helped me deal with everyday stress, and I learned in November and December, eight months into my fitness program, that it could help me deal with major stress, too. You are probably thinking that I already had my share of major life stressors, but believe it or not, four new ones hit hard and without warning.

Stressor #1

Mom, Elliott, and I have to get up long before light to get to school on time. One dark Tuesday morning as we drove through a residential area, we heard what sounded like a loud, sudden clap of thunder. Our car jerked and nearly wrecked. A full-grown deer had run into our car. I think the deer wreck was worse because it was dark outside and we had no warning before the crash. Mom, Elliott, and I were all shaking after the collision.

We could see the deer lying on the side of the road, obviously dead. We drove cautiously on to school. The sun rose as we pulled into my school, and we could see animal fur and blood on the driver's side of the car. We slid out the passenger side because the driver's side was crumpled. The rest of the day, we were all understandably stressed.

After checking out the accident scene that afternoon, I couldn't wait to get to the Y and let the U.S. Marine Corps take over my training. Mom said to relax, the accident had not been our fault, and next time we'd be watching on every dark road for runaway deer.

Stressor #2

Mom got the three repair estimates required by the insurance company. On Friday, she planned to drop Elliott and me at our schools and head for the insurance company with the estimates. I'd been up late finishing a school assignment, so I was sleeping in the backseat as I rode to school, with a blanket over my head. A few blocks from the school, we approached a four-way stop. Mom stopped completely, waited until nothing was coming, and drove into the intersection. *Bam!* For the second time in a week, a car crash shook our world. A car came over a hill and drove right through the intersection without stopping. We T-boned the other car and wrecked the front of ours. This time, the car was judged "totaled" by the insurance company, and in a few days, we had a new car.

The stress of two accidents left us all on edge. We lived with that uneasy feeling that trouble—the type that wasn't our fault and we were helpless to prevent—was around every corner. My stress was heightened, but I still had no interest in feeding my stress through food. All I could think was: *get to the gym.*

Stressor #3

About a week after Mom got the new car, she said she had to run to the mall. It was a dull rainy day, so I decided to stay home and work on my computer. About an hour later, Mom called to tell me she and Elliott had been in a third accident. A seventeen-year-old girl tried to do a U-turn in front of them and skidded her pickup truck on the wet road. The entire front end of the new car was crumpled, and we were back in a rental car.

Mom always sees a positive side to life, and she laughingly told us that our share of disasters was over. It was now a few weeks before Christmas and time to focus on the reason for the season. I kept up my cardio and strength exercises, and even with the added stress, I was okay.

Major Stressor #4

On December 12, Mom dropped Elliott and me off at school and said she'd have the tree up and the gifts all in place when we got home that day. Elliott and I were both excited. We'd planned to attend the Wednesday evening service at our church, but Elliott said he wasn't feeling well. We went straight home after school without even going to the Y. That decision turned out to be huge because we got home a few minutes before 4:00 PM instead of long after dark.

Mom placed the key in the front lock and pushed open the door. The security alarm was sounding at top decibels. She opened the door a little wider and screamed. Across a mirror in the foyer someone had spray painted a threat to kill the family cats. Beyond that, we saw what looked like a war zone.

Mom pulled the door shut and told us to wait outside until the police came. Elliott and I paced and Mom cried. We realized that what mattered more than our material possessions was the safety of our family pets. Elliott and I had adopted two rescued cats that were brothers, and they were like family members. We always laughed that Elliott's cat, Mr. Whiskers, had his personality, and my cat, Taco, was more like me. We'd had Taco and Mr. Whiskers for two years, and we loved them. Each day, they greeted us at the door when we arrived home, more like two puppies than two Garfield-size cats. We scanned the windows, hoping to see yellow-green eyes staring out of black fur, watching as they did each day. But if the cats were inside, they weren't looking out the windows.

We later learned that vandals had been in the process of destroying the house when they saw us pull into the driveway. They broke out a back window, setting off the security alarm, and ran through the backyard. But as we waited for the police, we had no idea what was happening inside the house.

We waited outside, terrified that the vandals had killed our cats. The police arrived quickly, and they were great. They found the frightened cats, and one of the officers took photos on her phone to assure us they were okay since we couldn't go inside until all the evidence was collected.

When we were finally cleared to go inside, we were numb. Vandalism is one thing in a movie, but trust me, it's a thousand times worse in real life. Mom had bought Elliott a hammer for Christmas, and the vandals had used it to bust every piece of furniture. They kicked in walls, knocked down the rails going up the stairs, and spray painted obscenities everywhere. They found paint Mom had bought to touch up the walls and poured it on the carpet. They destroyed our Christmas tree, stole our gifts, and even stole the food from the pantry.

We rushed upstairs to check our bedrooms. I always leave my bedroom door open because my many electronic devices need a cool temperature. But somehow my door was locked. The key was missing, and police had busted down my door to be sure the vandals weren't hiding in my room.

Apparently we'd surprised the vandals just as they started on the upper level of the house. They'd kicked some holes in the walls and spray painted Mom's and Elliott's rooms, but the furniture was undamaged.

After a minute, Mom, Elliott, and I all ended up at the foot of Mom's bed, staring at the wall in front of us. The vandals had painted: "We Are the Grinch Who Stole Yo X-mas."

Mom laughed as she read the sign. She agreed that our situation was a lot like the children's story. These vandals, like the Grinch, thought they could steal Christmas, but they didn't know our family. We had each other. Taco and Mr. Whiskers were traumatized but alive. We came home early enough to keep the vandals from destroying the upstairs. Though the restoration ended up costing nearly $20,000, we had more to be thankful for than to stress about.

We were grateful we were okay, but for months after the vandalism, we were also a little nervous each time we entered our house. The day of the vandalism, our security alarm had gone off about noon, and Mom met the police at the house. They checked each room but didn't find anyone, so they told Mom the system had probably malfunctioned. Mom reset the alarm and left. Later, the police said the vandals may have set off the alarm earlier in the day, hid while the police searched, and then vandalized the house while the security system was activated. After December 12, each time we came home, we had an uneasy feeling that someone could be hiding inside our house.

I was uneasy, but I was also angry. I was furious that the vandals had caused Mom to be so traumatized that her hair fell out in big clumps. I was mad that things we'd worked hard for or saved from our childhoods were destroyed. It was hard to imagine anyone getting kicks out of destroying someone else's property.

If I'd felt so much anger a year earlier, I might have wanted Mom to make a trip through a fast-food drive-thru for double cheeseburgers and supersized fries. That option never surfaced. Before I realized what I was doing, I was clearing the rubble from the house. I lifted big bookshelves and carried them outside. I carried what was left of chairs, tables, couches, and big CRT televisions.

I worked for days, clearing out the house. On Saturday, I worked alone at the house for most of the day. After bagging and carting what was left of our belongings, I realized I hadn't eaten since breakfast. I was so weak I could hardly hold up my head.

My grandparents live just a few miles from us, and if I'd been in that predicament a year ago, I would have called my grandmother and asked her to bring me a sack of chili cheese burritos. This time, I asked if she would grill me some chicken and rush it over.

The more I carried furniture, the stronger and more in control I became. And the more I relaxed. The afternoon the house

READER/CUSTOMER CARE SURVEY

We care about your opinions! Please take a moment to fill out our online Reader Survey at **http://survey.hcibooks.com**.
As a **"THANK YOU"** you will receive a **VALUABLE INSTANT COUPON** towards future book purchases
as well as a **SPECIAL GIFT** available only online! Or, you may mail this card back to us.

(PLEASE PRINT IN ALL CAPS)

First Name _____ MI. _____ Last Name _____

Address _____ City _____

State _____ Zip _____ Email _____

1. Gender
☐ Female ☐ Male

2. Age
☐ 8 or younger
☐ 9-12 ☐ 13-16
☐ 17-20 ☐ 21-30
☐ 31+

3. Did you receive this book as a gift?
☐ Yes ☐ No

4. Annual Household Income
☐ under $25,000
☐ $25,000 - $34,999
☐ $35,000 - $49,999
☐ $50,000 - $74,999
☐ over $75,000

5. What are the ages of the children living in your house?
☐ 0 - 14 ☐ 15+

6. Marital Status
☐ Single
☐ Married
☐ Divorced
☐ Widowed

7. How did you find out about the book?
(please choose one)
☐ Recommendation
☐ Store Display
☐ Online
☐ Catalog/Mailing
☐ Interview/Review

8. Where do you usually buy books?
(please choose one)
☐ Bookstore
☐ Online
☐ Book Club/Mail Order
☐ Price Club (Sam's Club, Costco's, etc.)
☐ Retail Store (Target, Wal-Mart, etc.)

9. What subject do you enjoy reading about the most?
(please choose one)
☐ Parenting/Family
☐ Relationships
☐ Recovery/Addictions
☐ Health/Nutrition

☐ Christianity
☐ Spirituality/Inspiration
☐ Business Self-help
☐ Women's Issues
☐ Sports

10. What attracts you most to a book?
(please choose one)
☐ Title
☐ Cover Design
☐ Author
☐ Content

TAPE IN MIDDLE; DO NOT STAPLE

NO POSTAGE
NECESSARY
IF MAILED
IN THE
UNITED STATES

BUSINESS REPLY MAIL

FIRST-CLASS MAIL PERMIT NO 45 DEERFIELD BEACH, FL

POSTAGE WILL BE PAID BY ADDRESSEE

Health Communications, Inc.
3201 SW 15th Street
Deerfield Beach FL 33442-9875

FOLD HERE

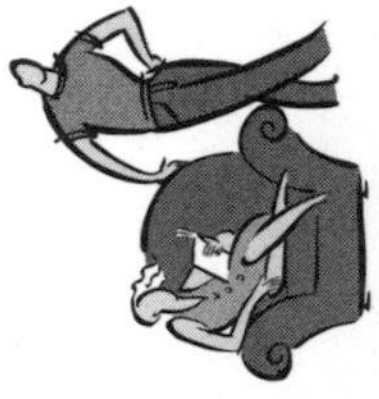

Comments

was finally cleaned out and ready for the restoration company, I sat on the front step and wiped the perspiration from my face. At that moment, I realized I was learning to substitute exercise for food. I felt powerful.

We spent the next seven weeks in a motel, and I discovered another pitfall of the vandalism. With any change of schedule, there's a danger of forgetting to exercise or eat healthy. The complimentary motel breakfast was a carb lover's delight: cinnamon rolls, bagels, grits, and cereal. I found a few healthy choices and refused to let myself go near the enemy foods.

And I actually lost weight. I went from a 40-waist pants to a 38 and then to a 36, all during the time in the motel. The families at my school donated $1,000 in restaurant gift cards to show their support, and Mom and Elliott ate out every night. I only went with them twice, when they were going to healthy restaurants. The other nights, I used the motel fitness room while they were eating. I either microwaved salmon or a healthy frozen dinner, or I asked Mom to bring me back a salad.

If all those things had happened early in my fitness program, before healthy eating and regular exercise were habits, I probably wouldn't have handled the stress as easily. But by the time I faced the big stressors, my new fitness program was a part of who I was.

The first time I experienced a series of stressful events—a murder in our family, a house fire, and Mom's divorce—I turned to food for comfort and ended up at my heaviest weight. When the second round of stress hit—three car accidents and vandalism—I discovered that exercise is a much more powerful stress antidote than food.

Stress will always be an obstacle in UFG. I've had some unusual stresses in my life, and there are probably plenty more in my future. It's not the stresses that count, since we all have our share. It's how we handle them.

We all need stress busters. If we don't find a way to deal with stress, our bodies will. That's how stress-related diseases develop. So my approach is to face stress head on instead of forcing my body to handle it. If I'm stressed, I work out to cadences. I imagine that I'm running down a track with a platoon of marines or airborne troopers. I feel like I'm in the middle of a battle, and in a way I am. I'm battling for good health. Running to cadences makes me feel more powerful than my stress. I feel like I'm rushing into a burning building to rescue a girl or I'm leading my troops into combat. Hooah!

I honestly don't think about using food to deal with stress. That may be hard to understand if you've never been seriously overweight. But I've come too far to turn back. I'll always have a little fear of becoming what I was, and that fear keeps me in line.

I've only cheated once in the past two years. Someone offered me a bite-size Butterfinger candy bar last Halloween, and I thought, *Sure. Why not?* I soon knew why that bite-size enemy had no place in my new lifestyle. It tasted good in my mouth, but as soon as I swallowed it, I realized it wasn't worth it. I'd come too far and made too drastic of a change to let a piece of candy ruin all my hard work.

6

Being All I Can Be

Fourteen months after I began playing the Ultimate Fitness Game (UFG), my first year at Chrysalis Experiential Academy was coming to an end. I'd never closed a school year with anything but eagerness for the long, lazy days of summer, but Chrysalis was different. It was more like a family, and I knew I'd miss Richard, our school's director; my teachers; and my friends during the vacation months. The end-of-school activities were mixed with a little sadness, but triumph was my primary feeling on that last day of school. This was the year I'd grown academically and shrunk physically. A year of milestones . . .

FINALLY, PROGRESS

A couple of us guys decided that we would wear suits on the last day of school. It was awards day, and we thought it would be fun to dress up. I had a nice suit, but I hadn't worn it in a year. It was a size 48, but I had some newer pants I'd gotten for a recent photo, so I figured I was set.

The day before school was out, Mom suggested that I try on my white dress shirt to make sure all the buttons were secure before she ironed it. I'd gotten a cool dress shirt with cuff links in December when we had mock job interviews at school, so I found it in the back of my closet and slipped it on for Mom to inspect. As I fastened the buttons, Mom and I stared silently at each other.

"We better make a run to the store," said Mom with a huge smile. The shoulders of the shirt sagged so far that the sleeves were past my knuckles.

It felt incredible to buy a size-medium dress shirt, and I thought my "problem" was solved—that is, until the next morning. I put on my new shirt and pulled the tie tight. Then I went to the closet to get my suit. The 34-waist dress pants were too loose, so I pulled my belt tighter and they looked fine. I didn't worry about the jacket. I figured a jacket could be a little loose and still work. I was wrong. The size-48 jacket made me look like a little kid dressing up in his dad's clothes. The padded shoulders stuck out far beyond my body. The sleeves nearly covered my hands. I could easily have stuffed a pillow inside the coat with me.

I looked comical, but I wanted to wear a suit, so I wore the only suit I had. All day I felt like I was carrying around giant rolls of fabric. My oversized suit jacket was actually heavy, and it wadded up beneath me when I sat down. Everyone thought it was hilarious, and it was fun to be laughed at for having a too-big jacket instead of having someone saying, "Whoa, dude. You need a bra."

I didn't want to wear the oversized jacket to our awards program that evening, but I still wanted to wear a suit. I knew we didn't have time to shop, so I thought of who might have something I could borrow. My granddad has always been thin, and, at six feet tall, he wears a size-40 jacket. I was almost as tall as Granddad, so I hoped something he had would fit. I still had no idea what size I wore, but even a too-small jacket would be better than the yards of extra fabric I'd lugged around all day.

That afternoon, I called to ask if Granddad had a dark suit I could borrow. He said he had a black blazer that should match my black pants. He promised to bring it when we ate out that night. My great-grandmother was visiting, and our family met for supper at a local restaurant. I entered the restaurant in my 34-inch waist pants, now pulled together with a belt to keep them from sagging, my size-medium shirt, and my handy dandy one-size-fits-all tie. After we ate, I walked with my grandmother to her car to get Granddad's jacket. I still remember the exhilaration when I slipped on the jacket and heard my grandmother say, "It's a little big, but it will be okay for tonight."

A little big. That meant I actually wore a 38. From 48 to 38 in fourteen months! The feeling was indescribable.

FINALLY, REWARDS & GOOD PROBLEMS

That night at the banquet, I was fortunate to win some awards. As my teacher, Jason, announced one of them, he said, "This goes to someone who always has a positive attitude, always has a smile on his face, and dresses sharp every day."

I never would have heard those words the year before. I'd always kept a positive attitude and usually a smile, even when I wasn't feeling that great about myself. But I usually wore black T-shirts, hanging out, and loose jeans as I tried to look smaller and more invisible.

Now I enjoy dressing up, but I still have my wardrobe

problems. Since losing half my body weight, my biggest problem is finding clothes small enough for my tall frame. When I bought some size-small elastic-waist khaki shorts to replace my old workout shorts, they slipped down so far when I exercised that I had to give them to a friend. When I order specialty T-shirts online, sometimes the only choices are large and extra large, and a size large looks oversized on me now. Never in my wildest dreams did I think I'd have trouble finding clothes that were small enough, but that's my new problem.

Another "problem" is getting a good workout. When I started exercising, 10 minutes on a stationary bike would raise my pulse to 190, and I'd have to quit. You need a pulse of about 120 to get a good workout, and now I have to run 6 mph for 30 minutes to raise my pulse to 120.

FINALLY, A WIDE-OPEN FUTURE

Once I thought my career options were limited. I told myself I'd never be an athlete. I'd never be in law enforcement. I'd never be able to join the military, and I couldn't be John Schneider's stunt double. Today, I enjoy sports. My granddad and I talk about the qualifications for an FBI agent, and I meet them all. Though John Schneider hasn't called to ask me to be his stunt double, I'm ready if he does.

I hope it doesn't sound like bragging to describe how tough I've become playing UFG. I'm just happy to be fit, and I hope that what I've accomplished can encourage others. I never forget how hard the climb was, and the successes only remind me how far I've come and how important it is to encourage others who are just starting out. I know the whole fitness thing is overwhelming at the beginning. Maybe hearing how drastically getting fit changed my life can be the incentive others need.

FINALLY, BUILT TOUGH

Each step forward, each small success, has encouraged me, and the memories of them continue to keep me focused on maintaining a healthy lifestyle. On November 3, 2008, my granddad and I took a trip to Stone Mountain to close out an important chapter for me. Together we walked 1.3 miles to the top of Stone Mountain. It's a trail of rough, hewn granite, and you're walking straight up. Our hearts were pounding when we reached the top, but we made it without stopping to rest. It was an energizing kind of tired, and it was something I hadn't been able to do when my class visited the monument two years earlier.

When we stood on top of that mountain, with very little body fat to protect me from the stiff breeze, I felt like Rocky Balboa when he climbed the last step of the Philadelphia Art Museum and threw up his hands in victory. I'd not only conquered Stone Mountain, I'd also conquered my DNA and the cravings that once made me feel powerless.

And just like Rocky, I was the underdog no one expected to win. I was on my way to a life of obesity, telling myself—and hearing others tell me—that I had no choice because I was born to be big.

Life changed for me when I lost 150 pounds. When I set out to get fit, my overall goals seemed big, but I realize now that they weren't big enough. I gained more benefits than I dreamed were possible. . . .

I wanted to run without being winded.

Now I can run five miles at full speed without gasping for breath. My typical workout includes lifting a total of 65,000 pounds on pulley weights (2 to 3 sets on twelve machines). I do 30-pound arm curls, twenty times on each arm. I bench press 90 pounds fifteen times. I pull up my own weight (145 pounds) five times. I do dips (pushing my weight off the ground) fifteen times. I low-row (a more difficult version of a rowing machine) 60 pounds.

Once, I had just wanted to run without struggling for breath. Now I'm strong. In grade school, kids always wanted to flex their muscles, but I was too self-conscious to show my arms. Not long ago, I arm wrestled someone at school and won. A kid standing nearby said, "Whoa, dude, you're strong." Those were words I never expected to hear.

I wanted to buy my clothes from regular shelves.

Now I actually love shopping (as much as a guy can). When you know everything in the store will fit, you don't mind trying on clothes.

Not long ago, Mom, Elliott, and I took a vacation day to Chattanooga, Tennessee. We rode the Lookout Mountain Incline Railway, and I decided to buy a T-shirt at the gift shop. Only large and extra-large shirts were displayed. I asked the sales associate if she had any small or medium shirts in the style I wanted, and she replied, "I think we have some small sizes in the back."

Once I was embarrassed when a salesperson reached into a

special drawer to get my XXL shirt, so that day I especially enjoyed hearing that my size—the small size—was in a special location.

I used to wear black nearly every day, and I still wear it a lot. Now I wear black because it has a powerful impact, not to hide my size. I also wear Hawaiian shirts, a yellow oxford, red T-shirts, and khakis and shorts instead of all dark jeans. Once I used clothes to hide my size. Now I use them to express myself.

I wanted to stop worrying about weight-related diseases.

Now my goal is total fitness. I know that no one is immune to injury and disease, but I'm confident that I'm doing the best I can to have a healthy body. When I began playing UFG, my goal was to protect myself, as much as possible, against type 2 diabetes, heart problems, and other diseases directly related to being overweight. But before long, I knew I needed a new UFG level. Now I do my nutrition homework and make sure I'm eating and exercising for totally healthy living.

This new level has actually caused me to include in my diet small quantities of foods that aren't super-low in calories or fat but are ones I need for a strong, healthy body—things like peanut butter, all sorts of nuts, pumpkin seeds, and sunflower seeds. I used to avoid anything with a high fat content, but now I realize I need omega 3 for a healthy heart and lower cholesterol. At first, I mainly considered calories. Now I know that some foods are worth a few extra UFG dollars.

I wanted to exercise long enough to work up a good sweat.

At first, I got my wish. When I started my fitness program, I perspired so much that I had to keep wiping my face and hands with a towel. But the stronger I got, the easier it was for my body to cool itself. Now I can run 20 minutes on a treadmill without sweating.

It's weird, but I miss heavy sweating. One of the most rewarding things after a workout is sweating so much your shirt is soaked. I love feeling that natural air-conditioning. That reward is getting harder to achieve because I don't work up a sweat easily.

I wanted to weigh 180 pounds.

I didn't really think it was possible for me to be thin. I just didn't want to be fat. But once the weight started melting off, I realized that I could actually be thin. That was an incredible thought for someone who'd spent most of his life being the biggest kid in the classroom. One hundred eighty pounds is average for my height, and while I don't want to take weight loss to an unhealthy extreme, I enjoy being described as "thin" instead of "average."

I wanted people to stop calling me fat.

I don't hear that anymore. My weight is right in the middle of the ideal range, and my BMI is 21, which is also in the middle of the ideal range. Because I exercise so much, people think I'm a lot thinner than I am. So now people tell me I'm too thin.

Not long ago, Elliott had an argument with a kid in the neighborhood. The kid called Elliott a few names, and, when that didn't work, he clenched his teeth and said, "Your brother is a skinny piece of doo-doo."

Elliott came home angry that the neighbor kid had insulted his big brother. I wanted to say, "Hey, tell him thanks for notic ing!" It's something I never get tired of hearing, and it's a description I still can't believe I deserve.

I used to wear an XXL T-shirt that said BUILT FORD TOUGH, and I felt like an imposter because my weight got in the way of being strong. Now I have a belt buckle with the same message. Though I'm not the toughest guy around, I know I'm tough.

I wanted people to see who I really was.

I wanted them to see Taylor LeBaron—funny, cool, talented, and amazing guy. Not Taylor, the big kid. And that may be the biggest change. People respond to me in a totally different way.

I love the reaction when I meet someone who hasn't seen me in a while. I keep up with my friends at my old school, and when they see my page on Facebook, they're surprised at the change. It's fun to hear all the compliments.

I'm now free to be Taylor, and that's great. But it makes me sad, even angry, that so many amazing people are being discounted just because they're overweight. It feels great to get compliments now. I appreciate people paying attention to what I say and wanting to hang out with me. But sometimes I want to say, "Hey, where were you when I was carrying around extra weight and needed some encouragement? I'm the same guy now that I was two years ago. I'm just inside a smaller package."

REMEMBERING I'M THIN . . . AND THEN SOME

No matter how far I advance in UFG, it's hard for me to remember that I'm inside a smaller package now. Sometimes I still think about myself as fat. I always wore a T-shirt with my swimming trunks, and I still can't bring myself to go to the pool in just my trunks. I won't wear muscle shirts or anything that highlights my body. Sometimes I feel like an impostor in the thin world and think that any minute someone is going to say, "Don't let Taylor on that. He'll break it." It will take a long time to erase the damage of kids' jokes and "he shouldn't be eating that" stares from adults at McDonald's.

But I'm finally thin, and one of my biggest problems now is forgetting that I don't have a lot of weight to brace myself. When someone hands me something heavy, I'm easily caught off balance. Sometimes when I pick up the weights at the Y, I stumble backward. I'm strong enough to pick them up. I'm just not prepared for them to be heavier than I am.

One day at school, someone handed me a computer server—one of the old, big ones that we were throwing out. It weighed a little over 100 pounds. I was used to having enough body weight to absorb picking up a heavy object. Without the extra weight to brace myself, I staggered. I'm having to learn to use my legs and my arm strength to balance myself.

While it's dangerous to forget that I'm now thin, it's just as dangerous to get caught up in being thin and let "thin" define who I am. I need to keep other things in mind, too:

I have to remember I'm still me.

I'm thinner, and I look a lot different than I did a couple of years ago. But I'm the same person I was when I weighed nearly 300 pounds. It's just that other people can see me more clearly now. Some people didn't take time to get to know the real me when I had the extra weight. I'll always appreciate my long-time friend Katherine. We've been friends since third grade, and she's treated me the same no matter what my weight was.

I didn't lose weight to become someone amazing. I lost weight so other people could see the amazing me a little easier. I didn't start living when I lost weight. I had a great time and did some amazing things when I was overweight.

I have to remember to be the best me.

Please don't misunderstand. It's great to be thin. If you're not there yet, let me tell you that it's even better than you imagine. But it didn't change who I was, and it won't change who you are. So while you're working to change the outside, start working on the inside, too.

Make sure that when people look at you after you're down to your ideal size that they say more than "There's a skinny guy." A new slim body is just the outside wrappings for who you truly are.

Did you ever get a gift from some relative and the package was wrapped like it was really something great? You couldn't wait to tear off the fancy wrapping paper and see the fantastic gift inside. But inside was . . . underwear. If you fix up the outside and don't work on the inside, you'll just be underwear tied with a fancy bow.

One of the ways I make sure I'm as "fit" on the inside as I am on the outside is to remind myself how I felt when someone made fun of me or pushed me to lose weight. That keeps me from doing the same to someone else. I also try to remember that the important thing about being thin is letting others see the person I've always been on the inside and making sure that my inner person stays focused on who I am. Thin is great, but it's only a small part of who I am. Keeping fit on the inside is just as important as keeping fit on the outside.

Being fit is both fun and dangerous. You can't let "thin" be all you are. You don't want your friends saying, "Hey, I wish the old you was still here. You were a lot nicer before you lost the weight."

I have to remember to encourage others.

I feel like, as a former fat person, I can do a lot to change people's attitudes about obesity. That's one reason I don't mind showing my "before" pictures. I have no intention of denying that weight control is my biggest challenge.

Not long ago, the Forsyth County Family YMCA, where I do most of my workouts, put up a poster of me in the lobby: a huge "after" picture with a small "before" photo in the corner. It was a little weird to walk by the poster each time I climbed the stairs to the workout room. I saw people looking at the poster, then at me, then back at the poster. I just smiled to let them know, "Yeah, that's me."

About the time the poster was displayed, a heavy-set man started exercising at the Y. He had more weight to lose than I'd had, and I hoped the poster would be an encouragement to him. One day, I decided to talk to him. I felt a little strange since he was older than I was, but I knew I would have appreciated someone encouraging me.

I told him I'd noticed him around the Y and just wanted to tell him that he could do it and that I was pulling for him. I wasn't just talking. I knew he *could* do it. So far, he's still working out. Some people watching him probably expect him to give up, but my bet's on him making it. I hope this man knows he has a friend at the Y. It's easy to feel like you're on the outside when everyone's thin and healthy except you. It's easy to feel—maybe correctly—that people are critical of you because you're overweight.

Probably as many individuals are prejudiced against overweight people as any people group. I read this on a teen blog not long ago:

```
"hey i dont like big people"
"be quiet!"
"Its the peoples fault that they are eating
too much. They need to have a balanced diet."
```

I don't think it's anyone's fault that they're overweight. Not too many people would choose to be fat if they could help it, so for some reason they can't help it. It might be stress or heredity or willpower. Whatever it is must be something they haven't learned to deal with—yet. But I believe everyone *can* learn to deal with their weight. I was one of the least likely people to take control of my health, so I know you can do it if I did.

I have to remember that I was once fat.

People sometimes ask me how I keep from gaining the weight back, and that's a great question. Ninety-seven percent of teens who lose weight gain it back, but I believe I'll be in the 3 percent who keep it off.

It's the memories that keep me from going back. I don't ignore the memories or push them to the back of my mind. I keep the 42-waist jeans—the ones I had to sleep in to make them loose enough to wear to school. I store my "before" photos on my computer. I remember the good-natured teasing from friends and the stares from strangers. Every time I run with ease I remember what it was like to be out of breath walking up my driveway. And I remember how deeply the real me was hidden behind an obese body and how people responded to the fat instead of to me.

I have an advantage in keeping my weight off because I have confidence and high self-esteem. I liked myself at 297 and 282, and I like myself at 145. My new body is just a nicer, more effective package where the always-amazing Taylor now lives.

I imagine that most people who gain back their weight are sending themselves the wrong messages. They're telling themselves they don't deserve to be thin, that they're destined to be fat. I tell myself just the opposite—that I'm now wearing the thin suit that I was made to wear. Change to a positive message, and you'll be more likely to keep the weight off.

I also imagine that people who gain their weight back are telling themselves that they have the option to stop exercising or eating healthy. I tell myself that there are certain things I wouldn't dream of cutting out of my daily routine—things like taking a bath or shower and brushing my teeth. I add my fitness routine to the activities I'd never dream of dropping from my daily routine. I never ask myself if I should brush my teeth each morning, and I never ask myself if I should exercise or play **UFG**.

Some other things I do to make sure the weight doesn't sneak back on:

I weigh myself often.

While I was losing weight, I rarely weighed myself. I knew I'd get discouraged if my weight fluctuated, and it was fun to watch the dramatic drops when lots of time passed between weighing. But once I reached my ideal weight, I decided to tackle every quarter pound before it became a half pound. Now I weigh myself several times a week. Any morning that I find my weight up, even a tiny bit, I reduce the "money" I have to spend that day playing UFG. Usually one day is enough to get the scale back to normal.

I threw away most of my "fat" clothes.

I keep the 42-waist jeans and a couple of other reminders, but I don't keep a closet full of XXL shirts that I can fall back on if I regain the weight. That would be sending my subconscious a message that I am planning to return to supersize. Self-coaching is crucial to keeping my weight off, and I tell myself that I'll never need those big clothes so I should give them to someone who's still struggling with their weight.

I keep good food company.

I don't hang out near unhealthy foods, and I make sure there's always something healthy to eat. Healthy foods don't have to be expensive—sometimes I just eat a plain slice of whole-grain bread or a serving of beans if I get hungry. And most healthy foods are actually as cheap or cheaper than junk foods. Meal-replacement protein bars seem expensive at two or three dollars, but a sandwich, fries, and drink from a fast-food dollar menu cost as much and don't advance my progress in **UFG**.

I keep up the cadences.

The U.S. Marine Corps never ceases to inspire me. I guess I'll be a career exercise Marine. But for variety, I've now added cadences from other military branches. The fast, steady rhythm of cadences keeps me running at top speed, and the messages encourage me to keep going.

I guard against the two easiest ways to slip from a fitness program.

One way is to simply decide to stop. The other is to gradually lose your discipline.

Deciding to stop eating healthy and exercising just aren't options, any more than eliminating other parts of my necessary daily routine. For me, a bigger temptation would be to gradually change the game rules. It's easy to tell myself that a little sauce or a smear of mayonnaise won't make a difference. It's tempting to shake the cereal box an extra time and pour out another half serving. Tracking my calorie expenses with **UFG** helps me face the little calorie amounts that can add up to extra pounds.

I serve as my own personal trainer.

I talk to myself just like I'd talk to a friend who's struggling with his weight. When I'm tempted to eat a cookie, packaged dessert, or mac and cheese, I tell myself to find a healthy alternative. Or I tell myself, "You just got into size-30 jeans. You don't want to go back to a 32."

I tell myself, "Look what you've earned. Look how hard you've worked and look at the results. You've worked too hard to throw away everything for a couple of cookies. You can have a sandwich for the same calories as two cream-filled cookies. The sandwich will be better fuel for your body to go running."

I'm surprised at how effective self-coaching can be (more about that in Chapter 10). It's hard to grab a couple of cookies when your inner voice is coaching you to eat healthy and stay fit.

I go through the motions.

Some days I stay at school past 5:00 PM for extracurricular activities and then I have plenty of homework. I want to skip the Y, go straight home, eat supper, and veg out. But as soon as I change into my workout clothes and start my cadences, I'm okay, so the key is to go to the Y regardless. Even if I'm falling asleep on the way to the Y, it all changes when I get inside.

It helps that my workout partner is now my mom, and Elliott is getting involved in the program, too. It's easy to stop by the YMCA on our way home instead of having to get out again later.

I keep food out of the spotlight.

I never let food be the focus of fun with my friends, a boring day with nothing to do, or even a birthday celebration. Keeping food in perspective helps me keep it under control. Food isn't my comfort, my stress reliever, or my entertainment.

I've found other people and activities to fill these needs. Food is fuel, and its main purpose is to provide energy for exercise and a strong body.

For my sixteenth birthday, my family knew I wasn't interested in cake, so they surprised me with a 16-foot sub sandwich, complete with sixteen candles. A couple of months later, Mom turned forty and we surprised her with a fruit cake—actual fruit stacked pyramid style with a candle on top. (By the way, six months earlier, Mom had joined me in my fitness program and had already lost more than 60 pounds, which has now become 75!)

I keep myself in the spotlight.

Everyone knows my commitment to staying fit: family, friends, teachers. I know they're all watching what I eat and how faithful I am to my exercise program. The people in my life would be shocked if they saw me eating a big wedge of cake or a candy bar. Knowing I'm being watched keeps me careful.

I savor the rewards.

Sometimes I remember the worst things about being fat—squeezing into a desk, not fitting through the window of Mom's car, the teasing—and those memories keep me focused on fitness. But just as often I remind myself how great it is to be thin. I think about the compliments and encouragements. I remember how good it is to walk into a store and find my size on the regular rack.

I have a lot of positive memories that are sort of like snapshots—quick pictures I can pull out of my memory to encourage me. Here are some of my favorites:

→ The afternoon I slipped into Elliott's jeans and they fit. I felt powerful, and I can feel that power every time I pull out this snapshot.
→ The day I ran 30 seconds at 6 mph on the treadmill. The first time I ran five miles without stopping. The first time I used free weights.
→ The day I borrowed Granddad's sports coat and it was too big.
→ When I reached the top of Stone Mountain and realized I'd conquered a mountain.

That's a little wallet-size album of mental pictures that I carry with me at all times. If I ever feel like giving food too big a place in my life, I just pull out the album and reexperience any of these moments. Thin feels better than I ever imagined. And no sausage and cheese biscuit can equal the satisfaction of knowing that you're in control of your body instead of the other way around.

I face the future with confidence.

Not long ago, I faced a new health-related crisis. I was feeling tired, and I was a little alarmed that my pulse was abnormally low. I checked a couple of Internet sites and found that an average pulse rate for someone my age is 60 to 100. My resting pulse was 40 to 42. My grandmother's resting pulse is in the high 40s, so I considered the possibility that a low pulse was hereditary and my extra weight had kept my naturally low pulse high. But 42? That was low.

I asked Mom to take me to Dr. Bagheri's. I'd avoided blood work when I was overweight, but now I asked for a complete checkup. Every test result was excellent. I showed Dr. Bagheri a copy of my diet, and he approved it without changes. The only thing left to check was my heart, so Dr. Bagheri sent me to a cardiologist.

I spent forty-eight hours hooked up to a computerized monitor. I dragged all my wires with me to my workouts, then unhooked the wires on Friday afternoon and spent the weekend waiting for my Monday appointment with the cardiologist. I imagined all sorts of heart ailments, and I wondered whether I'd still be able to exercise.

Over the weekend, I remembered *The Biggest Loser* episode where the medical experts put a model of a heart into a tub with 100 pounds of pig fat. If I had to have open-heart surgery, at least doctors could get to my heart easily. My fitness program would have given me an unexpected advantage. I'd been afraid I was damaging my health when I was overweight. If I had, or if I had a congenital heart condition, at least I was better prepared for surgery.

On Monday afternoon, the cardiologist put me on a treadmill to measure my heart rate. I had to run a long time to get my pulse to 70, but when I did, the technician said I could stop. Then the cardiologist examined the treadmill test and the printout from my two days of monitoring.

He gave me a diagnosis: extreme fitness.

Because of my intense exercise program, my pulse was well below "normal." When it drops too low, I feel tired. The doctor suggested a little more salt in my diet and a little more caffeine. Adding another Coke Zero or two to my diet was like getting a salary bonus.

The cardiologist wants to see me one more time in six months to double-check that my extremely low pulse is simply a combination of heredity and a healthy lifestyle. I expect another good report. But if I ever need surgery of any kind, I'm grateful the surgeon won't be cutting through layers and layers of fat.

Someone asked me not long ago if I planned to stop playing **UFG** now that I'm thin. I had no trouble answering, "Never." It would probably be easier for someone who had only lost twenty pounds and made a small difference to decide to quit. But my life has done a one-eighty since I started playing **UFG**. I was headed for health problems, career challenges, social disappointments, and low self-esteem. Now I'm headed in the opposite direction, and I'm excited about the possibilities. Why *wouldn't* I make **UFG** my lifelong lifestyle?

Part Two

How You Can Answer the Call, Too

7

Are You Where I Was?

I'm excited about the change being fit has made in my life. I'm enthusiastic. I'm energized. It's like finding computers on sale for five dollars and stuffing my car full of them. But there's a whole warehouse of great buys, so now I want to call all my friends and tell them to get right down to the computer store. Then I want to stand on the street corner and make sure strangers know about the great deal. Losing weight and getting fit—playing the ULTIMATE FITNESS GAME (UFG)— changed my life, and I want to tell everyone who will listen that they can do it if I did it.

If you've read this far, you probably struggle with your weight. You may be 150 or 200 pounds over your ideal weight, and you may want to cut yourself in half, like I did. Or you may be 20, 30, or 40 pounds above your ideal weight—just enough to make people see the extra weight before they see the real you.

Wherever you are in your weight struggle, I've been there. Are you teased, even if it's just friendly teasing by kids who have no idea they're hurting your feelings? Do you try to hide behind the darkest, loosest clothes you can find? Are you and your ideas sometimes discounted because you're fat? Do you dread shopping for new clothes? Do you worry about weight-related diseases? Whatever humiliation or frustration you're facing, I faced it, too.

Have you stood back when you wanted to participate in a physical activity because you didn't want someone to say, "Don't let him on. He'll break it"? Have you come in last, lost the game, or had to stop halfway through a race or even a walk? That was me once, too.

If you've had these fears, feelings, and disappointments, you're not alone. In fact, you're part of what I call the 9 Million Club. Nine million U.S. kids and teens are overweight, and the problem is becoming global. You don't have some rare disease. You're part of an epidemic because obesity in kids has tripled in the past thirty years. The problem is so serious that the Centers for Disease Control and Prevention studies obesity in kids just like they study other epidemics.

The good news is that lots of people want to help when an epidemic strikes, and the increase in obesity has generated a lot of research. With the Internet, help is at our fingertips. And with 9 million overweight kids, you can probably find a fitness partner. We're in this weight struggle together, and we can get out together. I'm sort of like one of a group of POWs who dug through the tunnel and crawled back to tell the rest of the prisoners that he found an escape route. I'm here to say:

Follow me. It's a long, winding, narrow tunnel, but I guarantee there's light at the other end because I've been all the way to freedom.

You've been a prisoner of your own body too long, and it's time to break free. You can find a million ways to escape, but here's a nice tunnel that's already dug. Just follow me through to freedom. It's better than you even imagined.

You may still be wondering whether a lifelong fitness program is worth it. I guarantee that it is. You feel better. You increase your future career possibilities. People respond to the real you instead of the extra pounds.

If you have so much weight to lose that you feel discouraged before you start, I was there, too. I was once overwhelmed by how much weight I had to lose, and things looked hopeless. It took a year to get into shape, but compared to a lifetime of fitness, a year to get there isn't bad. And if I hadn't decided to get fit, by now I'd probably be lots heavier than I was when I started **UFG**. I'd be looking back and thinking, *If only I'd started a fitness program last year, I'd be enjoying my ideal weight right now.*

Imagine yourself a year from now. Will you be sorry you didn't tackle your weight problem earlier? I can guarantee that it will be better to be looking back and thinking, *The worst part's over. Now I can enjoy my new healthy lifestyle.*

If you do nothing now, a year from now, you'll either be just the same, or you'll be bigger. Is either of these options acceptable? Don't look back on today and wish you'd started the plan so you'd already be thin. If you don't choose to get fit right now, the year will pass anyway.

IT'S TIME TO GET STARTED

So where do you want to be a year from now, still looking for the magic quick fix or enjoying your new fit lifestyle? If you chose "a new fit lifestyle," here's what you need to start doing today:

Stop thinking of yourself as fat.

You're not. Your body is carrying around some extra weight—maybe a lot of extra weight—but you are a thin, funny, talented, amazing person behind the fat suit. The fat suit isn't you. It's a costume. And no matter how snug and comfortable it's fitting right now, you *can* take it off.

Focus on the advantages of being thin.

Make a list of the ways your life will be easier and better when you're thin. Write them on a sheet of paper so you can refer to the list anytime you think fitness isn't worth the effort.

How would your life be different if you were thin? What opportunities would you have that you don't have now? How would people treat you? Would you be healthier? Would you have more energy? Would you have a broader choice of careers? Would you live longer? Would people pay more attention to your ideas?

Can you think of advantages of being overweight? If so, write them down, too. Compare the two lists. Would you rather be thin or fat? Once you make your choice, you're ready for action. If you prefer to be overweight, accept yourself and enjoy your life. If you choose to be fit, read on.

Consider yourself amazing.

Start by realizing that you *are* amazing, and it has nothing to do with your size. It's your mind and your personality that make you unique and therefore amazing. If you don't think you're amazing *right now*, you're not ready to start getting fit. You have to think of yourself as an already amazing person who's hiding behind extra weight—a superhero in a disguise. If you follow the program, but don't think highly of yourself, you'll sabotage your own fitness. Your inner voices will keep saying, "I'm a loser. I don't *deserve* to be thin."

Tell yourself that you *are* a loser . . . or at least you soon will be. Change the message from "I'm a big loser" to "I'm a big *weight* loser."

Count yourself worthy.

Even if they never say it out loud, some overweight people tell themselves they don't deserve to be thin. It's not a matter of who's *worthy* to be thin. It's a matter of who's *willing* to follow a fitness program. That's just a yes-or-no answer, and it has nothing to do with worth. So give yourself permission to be fit.

Start feeling good about yourself today. Then lose the weight tomorrow. An awesome person is already there inside you. *You know him.* He's funny, he's smart, and he's amazing! You just need to give that incredible person the body he deserves.

Imagine yourself fit.

I believe that inside nearly every fat kid is a wacky, funny, energetic kid who wants people to see beyond the XXL T-shirts. How can people see beyond the fat if you can't? Start acting fit. Treat yourself like you're fit. Anticipate that people will treat you like you're fit. The more you live the part, the more "worthy" you'll feel. And the more worthy you feel, the more likely you are to stick to a fitness program.

Keep the mental picture of a fit and energetic you in your sights. When an athlete runs a 50-yard dash, he keeps his eyes on the finish line. He doesn't look down at every pebble and leaf between him and the finish. He focuses on the finish line—the prize—and his feet naturally take him there. If you worry about all of the obstacles—instead of the prize—you'll stumble. Focus on being fit. The effort is worth it.

When Mom told Elliott and me that we had a long road ahead to fitness, I was discouraged. But it was true. It was a long road. But I had a long road ahead of me as a fat teenager, too. The road to fitness was a lot shorter than a lifetime of obesity.

You really have nothing to lose by trying to get fit. A lean, fit body is within the reach of nearly everyone. Even if you have a physical restriction that keeps you from exercising, you can still become healthier by eating the right foods in the right amounts.

You don't have to do it overnight. Start with baby steps. I lost 15 pounds between when I weighed myself at my great-grandmother's and when I joined the Y. All I did during that time was start paying attention to what I ate, especially high-calorie liquids. Even if I hadn't lost anything during that time, if I'd just kept from gaining more, it would have been worth it.

Remember the old Chinese saying, "The journey of a thousand miles begins with a single step"? It's old and maybe a little hokey, but it's still around and people still repeat it because it's true. Take the first step. Then the second and the third. The longer you play **UFG**, the more it becomes a part of who you are. Eventually you'll be running at full speed toward your goal.

IT'S AN UPHILL CLIMB

If you want to get fit, you're bucking some pretty scary odds. In the United States alone, 9 million kids and teens are supersized. If you're a kid today, there's a 14 percent chance that you're overweight. When your parents were your age, they had only a 4 to 5 percent chance of carrying extra pounds. All kids seem to be getting heavier—guys and girls, all racial and ethnic groups, all levels of income and education. We're generation XXL.

With Americans spending $33 billion a year trying to lose weight, why are most of us heavier than our parents and near-gigantic compared to our grandparents and great-grandparents? What's going on?

I think it's because most of us are on a program that's the total opposite of good health. A good fitness program involves exercising more, eating less, and choosing the right foods. A lot of kids today are exercising less, eating more, and choosing the wrong foods. What's different about us and our thinner parents and grandparents? Read on. . . .

We're computer experts and cell phone junkies.

We spend hours playing techie games, downloading music, and texting friends. Each new electronic gadget that comes along makes it less likely we'll be outside riding our bikes or playing sports. Only half of American kids are involved in heavy exercise like sports. About one-fourth has light exercise like walking and bicycling in their daily schedules. The remaining fourth has no exercise to speak of. It's pretty easy to figure that most of the 14 percent of U.S. kids who are overweight fall into the no-exercise category.

We eat more.

We love to supersize it. Monster buckets of movie popcorn. Buy-one-get-one-free hamburgers. Big-grab chips. All-you-can-eat buffets. Even regular restaurant portions are so big that most of us don't know what a real serving looks like.

We make the wrong food choices.

About a third of us eat fast food every day, and that adds about 6 extra pounds a year to our weight. And we eat fast food five times as often now as our parents did when they were teens.

Less exercise. Bigger servings. Bad food choices.

IT'S A LONELY CLIMB

Considering all that, it's surprising that only 9 million of us are overweight. But I'll bet you don't feel like that many kids are overweight. I'll bet you feel as isolated and lonely as I used to feel. When I was an overweight kid, I felt like I was the only one around who wasn't skinny and active.

It's hard enough just being a kid. We worry about body image. We feel awkward every once in a while. When you add extra weight to the mix, the mix gets heavy. The life of an overweight kid can be so uphill that we don't take time to think about our futures. If we did, we'd see heart disease, high cholesterol, and diabetes. We'd even see job discrimination and maybe a shortened life.

A lot of things are piling up to make teen obesity a huge

problem that keeps getting bigger. And it's a tough subject no one knows how to address. We don't want to hear the F word (fat), and most people hesitate to use it. Since adults feel awkward mentioning somebody else's weight, and kids get defensive when they do, maybe the best strategy is to tackle fitness and weight control ourselves. It's our problem, and we're the best ones to handle it. Here's how:

Stop passing the blame.

It doesn't matter if your family's eating habits are poor. You can reduce the amount you eat and make the best choices possible from what's available to you. You can't blame fast food or supersized meals. Even fast-food restaurants offer a few healthy meals—and *supersize* is a choice. Computers and video games don't cause inactivity. You cause it by not exercising. You may have inherited the fat gene, but you're the one who decides what to eat and how much to exercise. The fat gene can be defeated. If you can't afford to join a gym, you can still exercise. If you're concerned about the cost of low-calorie foods, plenty are inexpensive. Steak's a good source of protein, but so are beans and egg whites. When you're ready to take responsibility for your weight, you're ready to get fit.

Right now, you may be a member of the 9 Million Club. No one *wants* to be a member, but the membership roll is full just the same. Some members break away from the pack and take control of their weight, their health, and their future. If *you're* ready to opt out, read on.

Say good-bye to supersize.

If the F word has described you for too long, just change what the F stands for. Change it from "fat" to "fit." Decide now to let "fitness" describe you—permanently.

Fitness is a lifetime commitment, and even the most effective fitness plan, like UFG, won't work if it's just a diet or a strategy to reach a weight goal. Fitness has to be a new lifestyle. If you're just working to lose weight, you may lose it, but your success probably won't last. You need a no-turning-back commitment to a life of fitness and good health.

No turning back means just that. You get off the fat track—in your thinking, your choices, and your behavior. You choose a completely different route for the rest of your life—the thin track.

Get on track.

Have you ever ridden on those old-timey cars at an amusement park, the ones that even a six-year-old can drive? Usually they have two tracks for the cars. You go in one direction or the other, depending on which car you choose. And once you climb aboard, the car rail that maps out your path keeps you from veering too far either way. If the car moves far enough to the right, the rail will bounce it back to the middle. Then, if it veers too far to the left, the rail brings it back to the center again.

Once you choose a car, the entire route is mapped out by the rail that runs between the tires. So you may as well relax and enjoy the ride. You're committed to the route.

That's the type of commitment you need to fitness—total conversion. Once you decide to be fit, consider it a contract you can't get out of. Stop giving yourself options. Tell yourself there's no turning back, take away every opportunity to opt out, and enjoy the ride. That means getting rid of your fat clothes, giving up dreams of eating a big wedge of cake, and not seeing the "end" to your "diet" when you've reached your weight-loss goal. Reaching your goal just means changing the game plan to maintenance. It's like phase two of the same game.

It's all about mind-set. The best weight-loss plan will fail if you consider it temporary. Imagine again that you've jumped on one of the old-timey cars at the amusement park. You're riding parallel with another car, and suddenly you see the other car veer off to the right. That's when it hits you that you're on different tracks. Even if you want to take the same route as the other car, you can't. You're committed. Your track is the only option. Just knowing you can't change routes eliminates choices. Once you choose a car, your route is decided for you. When you get the old-timey car mind-set, you no longer have to ask yourself, "Will I have a doughnut?" or "Will I skip my workout?" No use thinking about these choices because they're not on your track.

Once you choose the fitness track, you'll find that life is actually easier without the choices that once dragged you down. Every time I was faced with a fitness choice, I struggled. When I made a bad decision, I was miserable. Now, if someone offers me an unhealthy snack, I tell myself that I have no choice. Unless I want to totally derail and give up everything I've worked for, I don't struggle with my response. Everything is more black and white when you're committed to a lifetime track. I used to live most of my life in the gray area. Sometimes I was in the whatever, whenever eating mode. Sometimes I ate healthy. And always, I was faced with decisions—decisions that usually left me feeling helpless and guilty.

Of course, I still make bad choices every now and then, but since I'm committed to the fitness track, my commitment pulls me back on track, just like the rail pulls the old-timey cars back in line. And I never consider one bad choice a terminal derailment. I tell myself that I'm committed to the fitness track, and the rail I'm traveling on pulls me back on track.

Make a commitment.

Another way to look at fitness is like you're signing a legal document. If you bought a car, you'd have to sign a contract promising to make monthly payments till the car was paid in full. If you adopted a dog, cat, or pet snake from the humane society, you'd sign a legal document saying you were taking responsibility for your new pet. If you got married, you'd sign a marriage license.

Sure, you could get out of these contracts, but it would be a big deal to do it. And until you took the proper steps to cancel the deal, you'd be legally bound. The contract gives you a feeling of commitment and makes you less likely to opt out without some serious thinking.

Imagine that you're an actor and your agent gives you a contract for a big Hollywood movie. Once you sign it, you'd better show up on the movie lot every day. Otherwise, you'll probably be sued by the investors. Since so much depends on fulfilling your agreement, you're not likely to break the contract.

Or here's a final way to think about your commitment to fitness. Imagine that you and a friend are helping your mom move an expensive antique dresser. It's solid cherry wood, and it's heavy. Until you lift your end of the dresser, you can still back out. But once you pick up your end and your friend picks up the other, a lot is depending on your holding up your end of the bargain. If you drop your side of the dresser, your friend will probably lose his balance and fall. The dresser will drop. Maybe it will break. And if it does, you'll see your mom's dark side. It won't be pretty.

Imagine that your fitness commitment is like lifting one side of a heavy antique dresser. On the other side, lifting as hard as they can, are your dreams and future opportunities. They're depending on how well you keep your end of the bargain. If you drop your end, your opportunities take a hit. And no one will be more disappointed than you. That's the type of commitment you'll need to fitness.

As you play UFG, take your commitment seriously. Otherwise, you'll do a lot of work for nothing. You'll deprive yourself of some good-tasting foods. You'll sweat at the gym instead of playing video games. Then your whole investment will be lost when you decide to quit. You might as well deprive yourself of movies and electronic gadgets and put the money you would have spent on these fun things into a piggy bank—and then open your bank and flush all your money down the toilet. Fitness is a waste of time unless it's a lifetime commitment. Promise yourself that you'll no longer lose the same 20 pounds over and over. You'll get rid of them once more but permanently.

8

Your Plan of Attack

If you've made the commitment to a new lifestyle, it's time to be the First Person Shooter in the ULTIMATE FITNESS GAME (UFG). As you create *your* personal game plan, consider three things: food choices, food quantities, and exercise.

I know I keep mentioning these three game components over and over, but everything else depends on getting this part of the game right. Every video game has basic rules that the rest of the strategy builds upon. These three things—food choices, food quantities, and exercise—are the UFG basics.

CALCULATING YOUR CALORIES

To figure out how much UFG money, or how many calories, you'll need to lose or maintain your weight, start by figuring your basal metabolic rate (BMR). Remember, your BMR is the number of calories you'd burn if you stayed in bed all day. You can find websites that calculate your BMR for you. They use different formulas for guys and girls, and they take height, weight, and age into consideration. Since the calculation includes weight, be sure to refigure your BMR periodically. A good rule might be to recalculate after each 20-pound weight loss.

Once you know your BMR, you'll need to calculate the calories you'll burn during your regular daily activities—walking to class, sitting in class, working at your computer, exercising, and so on. The calories burned during exercise depend on your current weight, so the best way to figure out your total is to do an Internet search to find a website with a calorie calculator that lets you fill in your weight and your daily activities; www.inter netfitness.com is good. Or try searching for "calories burned during exercise."

Once you've calculated your exercise calories, add them to your BMR. Multiply that total by 0.1. That will give you the 10 percent of calories it will take to digest the others. Add this number to the total. This is the calorie total you'll need for the entire day just to maintain your weight. If you'd like to lose a pound a week, subtract 500 from your daily calorie total.

For UFG fun, turn these calories into dollars—one dollar for every calorie. Now, consider how to use your money to your best advantage, spacing out your food to give you energy all day and making sure you have all the nutrients you need for fuel.

MAPPING OUT YOUR MEALS

My doctor, Dr. Bagheri, went over my diet carefully before approving it. It's healthy and safe. But it's based on foods I like and foods that I have available to me. You'll need a diet that fits your taste, budget, and lifestyle, so you'll need to customize a basic healthy diet just for you.

Think about the types of foods you'll need for your fitness

plan. Remember that the quantities will depend on your BMR and your activities for the day. If you're playing UFG, start your day with an estimated amount of money (or calories) to spend. By the time school's out, you might need to adjust your total if you find that you can't work out as long as you'd hoped. But start your day with as close an estimate as possible.

Breakfast

Planning breakfast is a crucial UFG strategy. If you don't have a healthy breakfast reserved for morning, you're likely to grab the first cinnamon roll that calls your name as you enter the kitchen. Line up a healthy breakfast before you go to bed, or a high-carb breakfast will sabotage your day before it starts.

And who says breakfast has to be breakfast foods? Think protein and good carbs. That can easily be last night's leftovers, a frozen dinner, or a healthy sandwich.

I start my day with some good carbs, some protein, and some dairy for calcium. Sometimes I have leftover grilled lean beef, chicken, or fish. You can't beat a high-protein start for your day.

Eggs may sound good, but the yolk is high in calories and cholesterol. Products such as Egg Beaters are a great alternative. They're mostly egg whites. They have zero fat, zero cholesterol, and good-quality protein. You can even get Egg Beaters Whites, which are all egg white. That's where the protein is and the calories aren't.

With Elliott's appetite, leftovers don't always survive till morning, so my typical rush-to-school breakfast is whole-grain cereal with fat-free milk, along with a low-fat, low-sugar, pro-digestive yogurt. That's a fair amount of protein, some healthy carbs, and a nice amount of low-fat calcium. Sometimes Mom makes me low-calorie pumpkin pancakes, which I have with a little sugar-free syrup, and sometimes I have a whole-wheat bagel with a thin layer of fat-free cream cheese.

How can you adapt breakfast to what you like and can find around your house? Can you stake out some healthy leftovers, label them "radioactive waste" (if you have a kid brother, this is crucial), and hide them in the back of the fridge till morning? Can you stash some healthy cereal and milk where you're sure to find them in your early morning stupor?

Check out some of our family's favorite recipes at www. cuttingmyselfinhalf.com for breakfast ideas. Remember that breakfast can be anything that's nutritious. A bowl of Soup by Ruth with a couple of Turkey Gobbles can be as good a breakfast as Protein-by-the-Square or Sweet Pumpkin Pancakes.

MIDMORNING SNACK

I like granola bars. They're satisfying because you have to chew them a long time. Or sometimes I put a piece in my mouth and leave it there till it dissolves. That way, my midmorning snack lasts longer. A granola bar contains some healthy carbs and other nutrients. You can probably find a similar snack that will keep your engines running till lunch. I'm not a big fan of fruit, but if I were, I'd probably eat a small banana, fifteen grapes, or a medium apple.

If your schedule doesn't allow time for a midmorning snack, you might want to tack an equivalent in calories onto breakfast. The key is to keep from being so hungry at lunch that you grab the first high-cal gooey carb you see and call it lunch.

If you have an early lunch, skip the midmorning snack and create a midafternoon one instead. The idea is to space out your food intake so you're never hungry enough to eat recklessly.

Lunch

If you eat a school lunch, you can probably choose some good veggies, protein, and fruit. A salad is a good choice unless it's loaded with cheese and fried meat and swimming in creamy salad dressing.

It's easy to start talking with friends, get distracted, and then misjudge serving sizes, so I usually choose a Healthy Choice frozen dinner or leftovers from home, which I've already measured. The frozen dinners have meat, vegetables, and just enough fruit to count as a daily serving. If I bring leftovers, I measure out servings of grilled lean steak, salmon, or chicken with steamed vegetables and whole-grain bread. I drink a bottle of water and a Coke Zero.

What could you have for lunch that would give you controlled portions of meat, fruit, and veggies? If you have access to a microwave at school, consider a healthy prepackaged dinner, which is usually cheaper than a school lunch. And healthy leftovers—in carefully measured portions—are even cheaper.

If your school provides lunch, think about some of the choices you normally have. Which are best? Take a few minutes to plot out your best lunch choices. If you've been choosing pizza, bread sticks, and ice cream, head for another cafeteria line. If you've been packing two sandwiches, chips, a snack cake, and a sugary drink, you can quickly cut calories and increase nutrients by packing healthy.

Afterschool Snack

After school can be a fitness buster, especially if you've eaten an early lunch. The time I leave school varies according to after-school activities, and on days when I'm at school late, I'm weak with hunger by the time we hop into the car. On long days, Mom actually hands me a sandwich as I get into the car, and I eat it as we drive home.

It's nothing fancy—just whole-grain bread and three slices of lean turkey. No cheese, no mayonnaise. No pickles, olives, lettuce, or tomato. No mess, few crumbs. But it fills my stomach, and the protein and good carbs start working to give me energy.

If you're hungry right after school, don't resort to random eating. Each night, set out a snack for the next afternoon: fruit, raw veggies, a little whole-grain cereal, a container of yogurt, or a measured serving of a healthy leftover.

Time Out to Calculate!

As you go through your day, keep a running count of your calories. By the time school is out, you should be able to predict how many calories you'll burn before bedtime. It's a good time to subtotal your day's calories and plan your evening so you don't see GAME OVER printed across the screen before you finish this round of UFG. Nothing makes me more eager to work out than realizing I need to burn more calories to eat a nice supper. Armed with your adjusted calorie total, get ready to exercise!

Pre-Exercise Snack

Before working out, it's a good idea to have a power-packed snack. I like to eat a protein snack about thirty minutes to an hour before I exercise. This seems to give me the best recovery from a strenuous workout. The carbs I've eaten throughout the day are burned first. Then, when my muscle tissue needs rebuilding, the protein's right there, ready and able.

I usually have a low-sugar, high-protein meal-replacement bar with 28–32 grams of protein. Scrambled Egg Beaters or a couple of scrambled egg whites are a good choice, too, especially with a little salt, pepper, or chili powder added. You can also have leftover beef, chicken, or seafood as a pre-exercise snack. Other options are fat-free cheese, yogurt, or even a cup of beans (which, by the way, has as much protein as 6 ounces of steak).

Supper

Supper is when you settle your score in UFG. You can spend only the calories you have left, so your food choices and serving sizes depend on earlier food and exercise decisions. Before you walk to the supper table, know what you have to spend.

If you're a typical kid, you don't have a lot of say about what's sitting on the table when you get there. Since we all try to eat healthy, our family's choices range from good to fantastic. If you're the only one eating healthy, you may need to pick and choose from the dishes your family passes to you. Your supper choices may be limited, but you have to be diplomatic about what you turn down. Parents can be sensitive when they've spent time cooking.

I seldom want to spend calories on liquids. I usually choose either fat-free milk or water with lemon with my supper, depending on how wealthy I am in calories.

If we stop for supper on the way home, I know the best choices at all our regular restaurants. If I know we're eating out at a great steak house, I save as many calories as possible throughout the day so I can enjoy a steak, warm bread (no butter), and a double order of steamed green veggies.

We have a lot of reduced-calorie versions of our favorite foods, and I've shared some of them on my website, www.cuttingmy selfinhalf.com. I earn my keep by washing dishes, not cooking, but the cooks in our family tell me the recipes are easy. If the cook in your house will make a few adjustments, you can save calories without sacrificing taste. If not, maybe you can volunteer to be the chef every now and then. Talk to your family cook about trying some low-calorie dishes or learn to cook them yourself. It's worth the extra effort.

Supper may be hardest to plan since you're less in control; you sometimes eat at home, sometimes with friends or family, and sometimes in restaurants. When eating away from home, make the best choices possible, watch portions, and beware of the calories in sauces, condiments, and toppings.

If suppers at home are usually a problem, ask your parents about the possibility of having a frozen dinner with controlled, healthy portions instead of the family's fare. If that's not possible, do your best to reduce the calories in your family's meals.

The fewer major choices you give yourself the less likely you'll veer from the plan. Your typical diet could exchange 3 ounces of lean beef for 3 ounces of baked chicken or 3 ounces of broiled fish if these are your favorites, but don't just tell yourself you'll have "a serving of protein." There's too much chance of trying to classify pizza as protein. You'd have to eat two-and-a-half slices of cheese pizza at 650 calories to get the same protein as 3 ounces of baked chicken at 140 calories.

Vegetables, like meat, are healthy and relatively low in calories by themselves, but not when they're swimming in butter or floating in cheese sauce. If that's the way veggies are served at your house, ask your mom or dad to set aside a dish of plain veggies for you before adding the extras. If that's not possible, take off as much sauce as you can.

Bread is also healthy, especially whole-grain, and it helps you feel full. But butter, cheese, and mayonnaise can double your calories with very little added satisfaction.

That leaves dessert. Fruit is good. No-fat, no-sugar pudding made with fat-free milk is delicious. Just about anything else is stepping into the danger zone. Calories from pies and cakes are mostly empty ones that don't give you fuel to exercise. They make you feel sluggish and bloated. And if you've eaten all the nutrients you need to be healthy and cut back enough to lose weight, there's not much chance that you'll have 300–600 calories in your back pocket waiting to be spent on a cake wedge.

Bedtime Snack

Maybe you just have an hour or so between a late supper and an early bedtime. Or maybe your family eats early and you stay up late finishing homework. Short time span, no problem. Hours without fuel, binge potential. You don't want to lie in bed, stomach gnawing, counting snack cakes instead of sheep. If you have a long span between supper and bedtime, you may want to save some calories for an evening snack.

All I have after supper is a bottle of water and a Coke Zero, but I'm so busy with history, Spanish, and statistics that it's not a big deal. It's actually easier to stick with Coke Zero and water than to make nightly choices.

If you need late-night fuel, I suggest taking the decision out of what to eat. Choose a snack (or two or three snack choices) and decide that's all you'll eat after supper. Choose snacks that are one serving, such as fruit, or individually wrapped, such as granola bars. Never spend your homework/TV hours eating directly from a bag, box, or jar of anything, even something low-calorie. If you choose a low-fat snack that's packaged only in a large box, check the serving description and count exactly the number of crackers, pretzels, or pieces in a serving. Take that number from the box and put the box away. You can even divide the box into individual servings and store them in plastic sandwich bags. I love low-fat Triscuits, and I know that a serving is seven crackers and 120 calories. When I need a snack, I pull out seven crackers and put the box back in the cabinet.

Think of food as fuel, not fun. Fun is taking a walk, not eating a pretzel. It's playing a video game, not downing a milkshake. It's talking to friends on the phone, not making friends with a milk chocolate bar. A lot of evening "hunger" is actually boredom. If you're truly hungry, eat a granola bar. If you're craving excitement more than food, start moving anywhere but toward the fridge. Exercise is the quickest way to get your mind off unnecessary eating. Once I started working out regularly, I noticed I no longer felt hungry late at night.

CHOOSING YOUR PERSONAL FITNESS FOODS

Before you can figure out your fitness foods and what amount you can eat, you'll need to know how much UFG money you have to spend throughout the day. So if you haven't calculated your BMR yet, get online and do it now. And if you haven't estimated the calories you'll burn on a typical school day, with only sitting in classes, walking down halls, watching TV, and doing homework, do that now. Check out www.internetfitness.com for a great calorie-burn calculator that lists most everyday activities. Other sites are also available. Do some research. (Here's a nice advantage if you have a lot to lose: the more you weigh, the more calories you need for basic activities.)

Now consider the calories you'll burn during a good workout. That will depend on what type of exercise you're able to do, how much you weigh, and how long you work out. Only you can estimate your workout calories, and you'll probably need a little help from Internet fitness sites. When you know your BMR, your standard activity calories, and your workout calories, don't forget to increase your calories by 10 percent to cover the calories used to digest your food. You might have something like this:

BMR: 1,850
Calories burned in standard activities: 200
Calories burned in a mild 20-minute workout: 150
Total: 2,200
If you want to lose a pound a week, subtract 500 from this total: 1,700
Plus 10 percent for digestion: 170
New total: 1,870 (the $ you have to spend in UFG)

Now, keeping your calorie total in mind, create menus using foods you enjoy and have available. If you have no control over what's available to eat, you'll have to do some fancy footwork to keep calories down, but it can be done. Here are some examples of how you can cut the calories in your family's everyday food:

→ If you are served pancakes for breakfast, have only one and skip the butter and syrup. That's 65 calories compared to 450 for an average sweet and gooey three-stack. You'll have calories left for fat-free milk and scrambled Egg Beaters.

→ Eggs, sausage, and biscuits? Choose only the eggs and save the 700-plus calories in two sausage patties and one biscuit, butter, and jelly (total for eggs, sausage, and biscuit: 950). Add a slice of toasted plain low-calorie whole-grain bread to two scrambled eggs for a 250-calorie breakfast.

→ Skip the mayonnaise, catsup, sweet pickles, bacon, and cheese on a sandwich. Instead, choose tomatoes, lettuce, onions, and mustard.

→ Choose lean beef or a baked chicken breast without the skin. If chicken is fried, peel off the coating and skin. The coating and skin more than double the calories, from 140 to 360. Drain hamburgers on paper towels (you'll save 100 calories for every tablespoon of grease you drain), remove every speck of fat you see (an ounce of fat is 250 calories), and make sure your serving is about the size of a deck of cards (yeah, I know that's small, but that's a real meat serving).

→ If your family has pasta, choose red sauce over white—or even salt and pepper or a little olive oil and garlic instead of sauce. And cut your serving size. Skip the garlic butter, but have a nice slice of plain Italian bread, and you'll feel satisfied and full.

→ The best vegetables are green ones (except peas). Corn, peas, and beans are good for you, but watch the portions because they're pretty high in starchy carbs. Here's a comparison of the calories in some vegetables to give you an idea of which ones to watch out for (the calorie counts are rounded up and are for a half cup, cooked).

Beans, pinto: 105	Corn, whole kernel: 70
Beets: 25	Green beans: 15
Broccoli: 30	Green peas: 60
Carrots: 30	Spinach: 25
Cauliflower: 10	Squash: 20
Corn, creamed: 95	Zucchini: 10

→ Beware of pie-crusts. Scoop out the goodies and leave the crust. A regular 9-inch crust like you find on meat or fruit pies is 950–1,050 calories, or 120–130 calories per slice (one-eighth of a pie). Double the calories if there's also a top crust. A graham cracker crust is just as bad: 850–1,050 for a 9-inch pie.

→ Baked potatoes are low in calories and high in vitamins and fiber. It's the toppings that will kill your UFG strategy. Try eating a potato with salt and pepper or salsa. Once you get used to the taste, you'll probably like it better than the loaded version. That goes for all foods without toppings and sauces. When you eat them plain you may actually enjoy the flavor more. You just have to retrain yourself and go through the motions until you start liking the natural taste.

You get the idea. If high-calorie foods are your usual options, there's still a lot you can do to reduce the calories per serving. And you can also reduce the serving size.

Beware of the "Invisible" Calorie

Every calorie counts, even if it's in an 8-ounce drink, in the mayo you spread on your bread, the sauce you pour over your pasta, the cheese you put on your sandwich, or the bacon you sprinkle on your salad. These are "invisible" calories, the ones you don't think about because you have them in small amounts. Well, these invisible calories are bigger than you realize. So when you do your calculations, remember that you have to count every calorie. As you tally your day, you may find, like I did, that some calories just aren't worth it. Add up the calories you normally spend on sweetened drinks, condiments such as mayonnaise and catsup, toppings, sauces, sandwich trimmings, salad dressings, and salad add-ons like cheese, croutons, and crumbled bacon. You'll probably discover that you can have another entire meal for what you're spending on these invisible calories. Like me, you'll probably want to save those calories for something healthy, satisfying, and filling.

Plan Your Menus

Considering your personal options, plan some possible menus. Write them in a notebook or in a file on your computer. Start by finding the calories in foods normally available to you by going to a site such as www.acaloriecounter.com. Use the sample worksheet on the next page to help you plan some UFG food strategies.

My Menu Planner

Breakfast

List at least two healthy, low-calorie breakfast choices that are available to you. List the serving size and calories for each food.

- _____ Serving Size: _____ Calories:_____
- _____ Serving Size: _____ Calories:_____
- _____ Serving Size: _____ Calories:_____

Midmorning Snack

Depending on the times you eat breakfast and lunch, you may need a midmorning snack. List some healthy snacks that are available to you. List the serving size and calories for each food.

- _____ Serving Size: _____ Calories:_____
- _____ Serving Size: _____ Calories:_____
- _____ Serving Size: _____ Calories:_____

Lunch

Lunchtime is a good opportunity to be sure you get in some fruits and vegetables, as well as some protein and healthy carbs like those from whole-grain bread and starchy vegetables. You'll want to spend a reasonable portion of your calories at lunch. List a few menu combinations that would typically be available to you. List the serving size and calories for each food.

- _____ Serving Size: _____ Calories:_____
- _____ Serving Size: _____ Calories:_____
- _____ Serving Size: _____ Calories:_____

Midafternoon Snack

Depending on your lunchtime, you may need a midafternoon snack instead of a midmorning one. You probably don't need both. Which is your longer stretch without fuel? The idea is to keep your body steadily fueled so you never get weak and you never get desperate enough to binge. If you prefer a midafternoon snack to a midmorning one, list some healthy snacks that are available to you here, instead of under Midmorning Snack. List the serving size and calories for each food.

- _____ Serving Size: _____ Calories:_____
- _____ Serving Size: _____ Calories:_____
- _____ Serving Size: _____ Calories:_____

Afterschool Snack

Think fast, accessible, and healthy. You're probably leaving school so hungry that you'll settle for any menu nightmare, as long as it stops the hunger pangs. The best way to avoid whatever-eating is to plan your afterschool snacks, limit your choices, and be sure your snacks are available immediately. List some healthy afterschool snacks you can grab quickly. List the serving size and calories for each food.

- _____ Serving Size: _____ Calories:_____
- _____ Serving Size: _____ Calories:_____
- _____ Serving Size: _____ Calories:_____

Pre-Exercise Snack

This is high-protein time. If at all possible, have a low-sugar high-protein meal replacement bar. If that's not possible, consider beans, egg whites, a drink made with a powdered protein mix, or another high-protein snack of 200–300 calories. List a few possible pre-exercise snacks. List the serving size and calories for each food.

- _____ Serving Size: _____ Calories:_____
- _____ Serving Size: _____ Calories:_____
- _____ Serving Size: _____ Calories:_____

Supper

Supper's the time to settle your score in UFG. Include anything you need to end the day with a healthy score. If you haven't had enough protein, now's the time. If you've scrimped on fruits or vegetables, this is your last chance before you sign off for the day and receive your final score. If you've saved enough money throughout the day, you should be able to buy a delicious, satisfying meal that will carry you over till tomorrow's new game.

List some healthy main course choices that are usually available to you. List the serving size and calories for each food.

- _____ Serving Size: _____ Calories:_____
- _____ Serving Size: _____ Calories:_____
- _____ Serving Size: _____ Calories:_____

List the vegetable choices that are usually available to you. List the serving size and calories for each food.

- _____ Serving Size: _____ Calories:_____
- _____ Serving Size: _____ Calories:_____
- _____ Serving Size: _____ Calories:_____

List the types of bread your family usually serves with supper. List the serving size and calories for each bread.

- _____ Serving Size: _____ Calories:_____
- _____ Serving Size: _____ Calories:_____
- _____ Serving Size: _____ Calories:_____

List any healthy dessert choices that may be available to you. List the serving size and calories for each food. (This one's optional.)

- _____ Serving Size: _____ Calories: _____
- _____ Serving Size: _____ Calories: _____
- _____ Serving Size: _____ Calories: _____

Evening Snack

If you're genuinely hungry at night or you have a long time between supper and bedtime, list a couple of possible healthy, hunger-busting snacks that are available to you. List the serving size and calories for each food.

- _____ Serving Size: _____ Calories: _____
- _____ Serving Size: _____ Calories: _____
- _____ Serving Size: _____ Calories: _____

Now that you've created your own worksheet, add up your calories for a typical day. How do your calories compare with the number you estimated that you'd burn when you calculated your BMR and daily calories? If you want to lose weight, your calories should be less than the number you estimate that you'll burn. If you want to maintain your weight, the numbers should be about the same.

If you need to reduce the calories in your menu, try trimming something from each meal instead of eliminating an entire meal or snack. If you space out your calories throughout the day, you'll have less chance of running low on fuel and serving up a big dish of ice cream for "energy."

Since the menus you're plotting will provide your basic nutrition, do a couple more checks to see how healthy you'll be eating. Calculate the carbs, fat, and protein in a typical day's diet. I try to stay at 90 percent of the recommended carbs, I keep my fat intake low, and I have at least 70 grams of protein. That doesn't mean those numbers will be right for you, too. Whatever rules you make for yourself, check to be sure the menus you planned fit what you need to lose weight and be healthy. Make any adjustments that will make your meals healthier and more practical.

Now consider your cravings. Your choices are to let them die of starvation or to feed them substitutes. Some people find that they can eat one piece of chocolate a day or drink one regular soft drink. If you do that, add those calories to your menu. I personally do better if I don't feed my cravings. I just tell myself that some foods aren't part of my UFG strategy. And the longer I ignore those foods, the less they tempt me.

But my craving for sugary drinks is still strong, and if anything could derail UFG, it would be soft drinks and flavored milk drinks. So I trick that craving with Coke Zero—my secret weapon in the UFG strategy.

Look one more time at your menus. Are the foods you listed ones you can easily acquire? At least one choice for each meal and snack should be something that's always on hand. You'll make bad substitute decisions when you're hungry, so stock up and plan. Then lock an emergency backup, such as a protein bar, away from hungry kid brothers.

Now ask yourself if these are foods you can live with. If so, lock them in. Commit to following your food plan. Eliminate any choices that aren't on your menus or can't easily be substituted.

At this point, you should have a basic menu. It's the home base for daily operation and exercise. Exercise is at least as important as food quantities and choices when playing UFG.

Hey, I'm a kid like you, but I've done my homework. I searched reliable Internet sites, my doctor approved my diet, and I met regularly with my YMCA trainer. I can tell you what works for me, but you'll need your own team of experts to help you. After you've planned your basic menus, ask your doctor to approve them. And, if possible, get one-on-one expert advice on what exercises are safe for you. Your doctor or your school nurse, coach, or health teacher would probably be willing to offer exercise advice.

It's always a good idea to get a complete physical before you start an exercise program, so if you've been avoiding the doctor's scale, now's the time to face your weight head on and ask your doctor for help. Start playing the Ultimate Fitness Game with your own personal fitness team.

CREATING YOUR EXERCISE PROGRAM

A lot of what you eat, how much you eat, and when you eat will depend on your exercise program. It's simple math: The more calories you burn, the more you have to eat to maintain your weight. And when you burn more calories than you take in, you lose weight. So to lose weight, cut calories and increase exercise.

I know I'm fortunate to be a member of the YMCA. Not everyone has access to a fully equipped fitness center, but everyone can find a way to exercise. You need two types of exercise: cardio and strength-building.

Cardio

Cardio means "heart." Cardio is intense exercise that gets your heart pumping and improves your cardiovascular system—your heart and blood vessels. To give your cardiovascular system a healthy workout, you need to exercise hard enough to get your pulse rate up to 150–160 for at least 20 minutes. That probably won't be possible at first, but make it your goal.

I do cardio on a treadmill, stair climber, or elliptical, but you can get the same benefits by walking (and later running) in your neighborhood, in an empty parking lot, or at the playground of a local elementary school. And if you live in a two-story house or an apartment building, you have your own built-in stair climber.

Start slowly and increase your distance and speed a little each time. Most treadmills and stationary bikes allow you to check your heart rate, and some even shut down when your pulse gets too high. But if you're walking in your neighborhood or climbing your apartment stairs, learn to pay attention to your body's stress signals. Stop exercising when you feel your heart beating too fast.

Learn to take your pulse. If you don't have a parent or teacher who can show you how, find help online. (An easy way to check your own pulse rate is to press your index finger on the inside of your wrist for 10 seconds and count the number of times you feel your pulse. Multiply this number by 6.)

Remember that your goal is a lifetime of fitness, so start off slowly and increase in small increments.

At first you can wear just about any shoes—I started out wearing boots. But as your exercise intensifies, you'll need good workout shoes. My workout shoe of choice is New Balance. They're strong, comfortable, and durable. Workout shoes don't have to be expensive, but they should have thick soles that absorb the impact as you run.

If you feel a muscle starting to pull or realize you're getting a blister, stop and regroup. It's better to miss a day or two as your body heals than to end up with an injury that stops your program for a couple of weeks. If you start out slow and increase gradually, you'll be less likely to have big or small injuries.

I love punching in my five-digit code when I finish working out at the Y and getting a report of the total pounds I've lifted and the distance I've run. But you can also keep track of your exercise in your computer file or journal where you planned your menus. If you have Excel on your computer, you can create graphs that show your exercise progress.

Go back to your journal or computer file. This time, create your own cardio plan, including a short-term goal and a starting plan. Right now, your short-term goal may be as simple as "walk once around my block" and your starting plan may be "walk to my neighbor's mailbox and back." By this time next year, your goal may be to run a mini-marathon.

Write your cardio exercise plan in your journal or computer file, including your short-term goal and your starting plan. (As you increase your strength and stamina, you'll want to revamp your goal and starting plan, changing to more challenging exercises and longer exercise times.) If you have a trainer, teacher, or other adult who can help you set goals, that's great. But you can also find expert help on some of the websites I've already mentioned, like www.WebMD.com, www.cdc.gov, www.heath vault.com, and www.ahealthyme.com.

Strength-Building

Strength-building exercise is the type that tears and rebuilds muscles. Lifting weights and doing pull-ups and push-ups are the best types of exercise for building muscles. I love the YMCA machines and free weights, but you can also strengthen your muscles any time at home with a set of 40-pound dumbbells, which cost about thirty dollars. They come with eight 5-pound weights. Add them one at a time as you gain strength. I like to work one side of my body at a time so I can now put all 40 pounds on one dumbbell and do intense arm curls any day I can't get to the Y.

You can probably find plenty of objects around the house that you can use for weight training until you can save up for dumbbells. For instance, a 2-liter bottle filled with liquid weighs about 4 pounds. Your starting plan could be to "arm curl a 2-liter bottle of liquid once with each arm" and your short-term goal could be to do ten arm curls with each arm. Other objects will work as well as a 2-liter bottle. Just be sure you can lift them with one hand.

Another easy strength-building exercise that requires no equipment is the wall push-up. If you're just starting an exercise program, regulation push-ups may be impossible. A great way to build strength early in your program is to do push-ups against the wall. (See "Wall Push-Ups" on page 141.)

Write your strength-building goals in your journal or computer file, including your short-term goal and your starting plan. If you're creating a plan without adult help, remember all the websites that I've mentioned where you can find expert advice.

PACING YOURSELF

Your personal fitness plan should be challenging but not discouraging. Those of us who have been XXL most of our lives are more likely to work too hard than not hard enough. But start-

Wall Push-Ups

Stand 2 feet from a wall. Put your palms flat on the wall, about 2 feet apart and at the height of your shoulders. Keep your back straight and your elbows in as you push away from the wall and then ease forward till your head touches the wall. Think of the wall as the floor and you'll understand how to do a push-up by pushing away from the wall and then easing back toward it. Wall push-ups are much easier than regulation push-ups, but they give you a good workout when you're starting your program. Your arm muscles will probably give out before your heart rate gets high, but pay attention to your body's stress. Start with a few push-ups and increase slowly.

ing slow is smart. The more weight you lose and the more you exercise your muscles, the easier playing UFG will become. Use the strength and energy you gain in the first weeks to make increasing the intensity of your program easier. The early diet and exercise changes may seem slight, but they're the tickets to buying a more intense program later. Diet and exercise are tough, and you have to earn your increases by being faithful to strategy in the early stages.

Think about it like taking a course in school. I'm taking statistics this year, and it's tough. But I just got my semester grade—an A—and it's fun once I grasped the concept. If I'd taken the semester exam the first day of school, I would have gotten a flat zero. But I have a great teacher, Chris, who's brought the students a little at a time to the point of actually understanding statistics. Chris took us to Starbucks one day and showed us how statistics work. We counted how much space Starbucks used to display coffee and how much space they used to display pastries. Next, we calculated the cost of the products and counted how many people bought both products. Then we mapped out the best use of Starbuck's display space to make the most money. After some fun projects like this, I'm getting the hang not only of how statistics work but, more important, how statistics can someday help me.

As good as I'm feeling halfway through statistics, I would fail the end-of-the-year exam if I took it now. I have lots more to learn, a little every day, five days a week. But each day, the final exam seems less threatening.

That's a whole lot like fitness. If we try to jump into the middle, or attack a faraway goal, we'll fail. But if we start out slowly and increase our ability a little each day, we'll soon not only figure out how to get fit but we'll also understand why it's important for now and for our futures. And that gives us the incentive to make the rest of our lives healthy.

After this year, I'll probably never take statistics again, but it will always be part of my way of solving problems. Like most things we learn, it will be part of who I am. Fitness is the same. For the first year, it may seem like your life revolves around getting the weight off and getting healthy and tough. But once you reach your ideal weight, fitness still needs to be a part of who you are. You won't be quite as focused on diet and exercise—they'll come more naturally—because they'll be your new "DNA."

9

Your Personal Strategy

It's important to get fit gradually, but you need an overall strategy to start playing the ULTIMATE FITNESS GAME (UFG). To begin, you'll need an actual time line. Have you ever had a teacher tell you on the first day of school that you'd have a paper due before winter break? You probably didn't get started on the paper that afternoon because the due date was so far away. Maybe you put the assignment aside altogether. Then your teacher reminded you in early December that the paper was due in two weeks. What was your response? If you'd spaced out the work over several months, the two-week reminder wouldn't have caused you any stress. It works the same way for UFG. It's good strategy to set realistic short-term goals and create time lines and deadlines for making them happen.

Another major UFG strategy is determining who you can turn to for support. No matter how committed you are to the plan, you'll need a backup team—allies in the game. We'll get to that later in the chapter. Rules are an important UFG strategy, too. From hide-and-seek to running for president, every activity needs rules. This chapter explains the UFG rules.

And finally, making friends with the enemy—in this case, food—is one of the most powerful strategies of all. It was my friendliness with food that made me obese, but I'll share my new food friendship in this chapter—the one that melted away 150 pounds.

TIME LINES AND DEADLINES

Unless you set deadlines now, you'll be disappointed next year when you're no closer to being fit. Here's a sample time line that may help you take that first step and keep pacing yourself to the finish line. Create your own time line in your notebook or on your computer, and record *actual dates* when you'll complete each action.

Strategizing

Do all of these things *before* starting your fitness program.

→ Make a commitment to change your lifestyle. Remind yourself that you're not starting a diet; you're changing the way you respond to fitness for the rest of your life.

→ Make a conscious decision to think about yourself as pre-thin instead of hopelessly overweight.

→ Finish reading this book.

→ Plan menus and exercise that fit your lifestyle and resources.

→ List the reasons you want to lose weight (health, appearance, friends, future career choices—list every benefit you'll experience).

→ Find someone to support you in your fitness efforts.

→ Plan a time and place to work out at least four times a week. Don't worry if right now "working out" means walking to the mailbox. Just be sure you're doing something.

→ Do some online fitness research. Bookmark sites for calorie counting, exercise, and healthy diets. Here are a few to get you started: www.WebMD.com, www.cdc.gov, www.health vault.com, www.acaloriecounter.com, www.internetfit ness.com, and www.ahealthyme.com.

→ Say yes to fitness, then create your strategies and think through how they'll operate. I use Marine Corps cadences for serious workouts and the UFG approach to monitoring exercise and eating healthy. Maybe you like these methods, or maybe you have a different idea that's perfect for you.

→ Estimate the calories you burn on an average day.

→ Choose the date you'll begin your fitness program. Write it on your calendar. Make a commitment to start your new lifestyle on the day you choose.

Starting

Follow this starting plan for a full two weeks.

→ Weigh yourself (only once as you begin the program).

→ Reduce your daily calories by a small amount, concentrating mostly on getting rid of the junk in your diet.

→ Begin a simple exercise program. Get your heart pumping, but don't overdo it.

→ Go back to the fitness sites you bookmarked and read a little.

→ If you're not using exercise machines that measure your pulse rate, learn to check your own pulse.

Increasing

Set dates for your first increase, then change the dates each time your body tells you you're ready. There's no realistic way to predict when you'll be ready to increase exercise or decrease calories, but try to tighten your program at least every two weeks. Keep challenging yourself.

→ Start implementing your unique program, such as managing calories and exercise through UFG, then increase the challenge every two weeks. For instance, give yourself less "money" to play UFG—in other words, reduce your calories some more. Since we're talking long-term fitness, I'd suggest taking your time and decreasing your intake by no more than 200 calories per week. Remember the wheelbarrow example in Chapter 4? If you move slowly, you'll hardly notice that your fitness program is intensifying.

→ Increase your exercise every two weeks, based on your pulse rate. Eventually, you'll want to raise your pulse to 160 for at least 20 minutes. If it gets above 190, stop exercising for a few minutes. (Speak to your doctor or a fitness trainer about this for more information.)

→ Keep track of your daily food intake and calories, as well as your exercise.

→ Spend time checking out fitness sites. Talk to people who support your efforts, either online or in person.

→ Weigh yourself no more than once every two weeks. Keep a chart of your progress.

Maintaining

When you're finally "tough as a nail and thin as a rail"—stay that way.

→ Weigh yourself at least weekly. When you reach that super state called Your Ideal Weight, how do you maintain that status, without gaining or losing? Now's the time to weigh more often and catch a little problem before it becomes an extra 10 pounds and steers you right back to oversized jeans and baggy T-shirts.

→ If your weight goes up even 1 pound, reduce calories and increase exercise until you're back to Your Ideal Weight. It's easier to lose 1 pound now than 10 pounds next month, so now is the time to be your own drill sergeant.

→ It may seem impossible now, but during the maintenance phase you may find yourself dropping a little too much weight. If you're losing a little more than you planned, increase your calorie intake a little. (Jelly doughnuts and milk shakes are not options.) Add an extra slice of lean meat, a double serving of green vegetables, or a bowl of whole-grain cereal.

→ Keep exercising. When your muscles are ripped and reformed, you can probably keep them that way with a little less effort, but you'll want to continue a regular exercise program. And you'll want to keep your heart healthy by doing no less than 20 minutes of cardio four times a week.

→ Eat sensibly. You've reached Your Ideal Weight. You are a thin person. But you're thin because you work at it. You're not one of those annoying people who can eat anything and not gain weight. You will always have to be aware of what you eat and in what quantities.

→ Arm yourself with self-coaching techniques (there's help in Chapter 10). If you think "just one" of a high-calorie food won't hurt you, remind yourself that these foods once made your life miserable, they are not your friends, and they won't hesitate to drag you right back to obesity.

→ Throw away the fat clothes. You are not going back there, so you don't need the wardrobe to live the fat life. Give them away. Have a garage sale and buy a YMCA membership with the profit. Keep just one giant pair of pants or a 3X shirt as a reminder of what life used to be and how hard you worked for your new existence.

YOUR BACKUP TEAM

Imagine that you get your report card. You've worked hard, but will the report show all the TV shows and video games you sacrificed to study for history and geometry? Your hands tremble as you open the envelope. All A's! Who's the first person you tell? That person is probably your Cheerleader. He or she has faith in you and expects you to succeed. It's fun to tell your

Cheerleader good news because you'll always get an "atta-boy."

Suppose you study all night for an exam and do your absolute best. But you fail. You totally bomb out. While the other kids are waving their A and B papers, you're looking for a trash can where you can bury your lousy grade. You need someone who understands your misery. Someone who will tell you to try harder next time but will also say, "I know you did your best." Who's that tough friend? He or she is probably the All-Weather Coach who challenges you to go a little further and work a little harder.

You fill out an entry form at a media store. The next week you get a call. You won the grand prize: a $1,000 gift certificate. Two minutes of filling out a form and you're the big winner! You grab your phone to share the good news. Who do you call? This person is probably your Party Guy (or Girl) who loves to celebrate.

Your mom tells you you're grounded the next time she checks your room and every flat surface is covered with junk. You get busy and forget. Who reminds you to clean your room? It's the person who's always checking up on you, reminding you, and making sure you get things done. That person is probably your Accountability Partner.

Maybe the people you thought of are family members: parents, grandparents, aunts, uncles, cousins. Maybe they're friends, kids from school, or neighbors. Maybe the same person came to mind for all the categories. The person or people who came to mind are valuable to your emotional health on an average day. You need someone to believe in you, to be your cheerleader. You need a coach who pushes you a little further than you think you can go. And you need someone who's ready to celebrate even your small successes. You also need someone to hold you accountable.

You're going to need all these people as you take on your new lifestyle and play UFG. You'll need someone to challenge you to do it, to say you can do it, to make sure you do it, and to sing your praises when you do. These jobs don't have to be done by a pricey personal trainer. That's a dream-come-true luxury, but a friend or family member can do the job, too. One person may be able to do two, three, or all of these tasks, but you may need help from a lot of people.

Choosing Your Allies

In the weight-loss arena, you may find that some friends and family aren't as supportive as you'd like them to be. They may even try to sabotage your plan. I understand, because when my mom tried to lose weight before I began my new lifestyle I did my best to discourage her. I realize now why I did that (losing weight seemed out of *my* reach so I didn't want anyone else to succeed), so I think I know where some of your friends and family are coming from. You're doing something they haven't been able to do.

Think about the people you identified as your best coaches and encouragers. How do they feel about fitness? Are any of them overweight? Do they have other bad habits they haven't been able to kick? If they have issues that keep them from being supportive, don't be upset. You might be the same way if the circumstances were reversed. But they probably aren't the best choices for coaches and encouragers.

After screening all your prospects, who's still in the running? Tell these people about your fitness plan. Ask them to hold you account-able to sticking to the program. If you tell someone on Monday that you're starting a healthy lifestyle, you won't want them to see you eating a bacon double cheeseburger and chili cheese fries on Tuesday. Just sharing your plan makes it harder to turn back.

If you think your usual supporters may not give you the help you need, you may want to wait until you're well into your fitness game before telling them what you're doing. When I started getting fit, I didn't tell a lot of people. Of course, my trainer, Dyan, knew, and Mom knew because she drove me to the Y. The rest of the family realized I was working out, but no one knew how hard I was working.

Enlisting Your Allies' Help

My family would have been supportive, but I just wanted to get started on my own. I played it low key until people started noticing my weight loss. I ate what was served for supper, scraping off sauces and gravies, draining grease, removing fat, and choosing smaller portions.

When I knew I was on my way to success, I was more open about what I'd been doing. It probably would have been easier if I'd asked for help and encouragement right away. As soon as my family realized how serious I was about losing weight, everyone pitched in to provide a lot of delicious low-calorie foods. I realized I'd been missing more than just encouragement.

After the rest of my family noticed I was getting fit, they made sure I had the foods I needed for UFG. I would have had a smoother start if I'd told everyone right away, but that's just me. One rule I think is important in any fitness plan: **Do what**

works for you, as long as it's safe and healthy. Some people enjoy tiny pieces of the foods they crave; it helps me to just stay away from them. Some people find morning exercise more effective and convenient; I like to exercise on my way home from school or even at night.

I could have had active support early if I'd asked for it, but I did have an unspoken support for who I was, with or without the extra weight. Knowing my family loved me, no matter what my weight, was the best support I could have had. No one pushed or embarrassed me, not even my doctor, but when I lost weight they were all there to cheer for me. It feels great to know everyone is happy for me. You need supporters, too, so find them somewhere.

Telling Your Allies What You Need

After you choose your supporters, decide what sort of help you'll need as you play UFG. Do you need someone you can call when you're tempted to eat something unhealthy? Someone who will talk with you till the craving passes? Someone to weigh you and keep your diet and exercise logs honest? Sometimes knowing you'll report your fitness to someone keeps you sweating at the gym or saying no to second helpings.

Or do you just need someone to say "way to go" when you reach a goal? Someone you can call, e-mail, or text when you lose a pound or walk a mile? Do you need help arranging healthy foods or transportation to a gym or elementary school where you can work out?

When you know exactly what type of help you need, ask. Let your supporters know what you're doing and what help you need.

You might say something like, "I've decided to get healthy. I know I've got a big job ahead, but I'm ready. I plan to start exercising, making better food choices, and eating smaller portions. I can't do it alone, though, and I wondered if you'd help. I need somebody to walk with me each afternoon. That will help keep me committed. Would you be willing to walk with me for about twenty minutes three or four afternoons a week? Maybe while we walk, I can keep you updated on the other things I'm doing to get fit."

If you know at least one person who would be a good encourager, you're headed in the right direction. If the person says yes, you're off and running. If not, keep looking. . . .

Finding Outside Support

So what if you don't have supportive friends and family? That's no reason to give up on your plan. You can find people, products, and organizations to be your support system. Your cheerleaders may even be online bloggers on fitness sites. Use your imagination.

Here are some ideas to get you started.

→ Google to find a weight-loss blog where you can post questions and celebrate successes. You'll find online weight-loss communities where everyone's working to do exactly what you're doing. I use www.yahooanswers.com and www.wikianswers.com to get answers from everyday people who may be struggling with the same issues that challenge me. And, of course, I double check with the experts on www.WebMD.com, www.cdc.gov, www.ahealthy me.com, and www.healthvault.com. Blogs are great, but they change so often that it would be better to find your own than for me to suggest my favorites.

→ Stay focused by watching TV weight-loss reality shows and fitness programs. They'll remind you that others are trying to lose weight and plenty are succeeding. *The Biggest Loser* is a popular program. I also like *Dr. Oz.* You can find others on network TV, cable, or satellite, so check the listings within your family's TV coverage.

→ Talk to a teacher at your school about starting a fitness group. You may find that other kids at your school are just as eager to lose weight. Some hospitals even have exercise groups to help overweight kids get started on a fitness plan without having to work out with a bunch of already-fit kids. Look around for groups like these that are sensitive to amazing kids who struggle with their weight.

If you're super self-conscious about your weight, the Internet and television help you stay anonymous. You can also use self-coaching (more about that in Chapter 10). Being my own coach and listening to Marine cadences worked best for me until I started to see results, along with—of course—my mom and my coach, Dyan.

A lot of what I did was based on general exercise and nutrition help I received from Dyan, but I used instinct and common sense to create a customized program that worked best for me personally. I was self-conscious about my weight, so I became my own coach, played UFG alone, and did solitary exercise. I had to work twice as hard when I served as my own coach, but it was worth it to me to prove I could lose the weight before announcing my plan. Family and friends can be your encouragers. Internet and TV personalities you've never met can hold you accountable with their tips and reminders. Or you can be your own coach. Whatever works for you.

RULES TO LIVE BY

Sir! Yes, Sir!

Most of us don't like rules, but what happens without them? Without traffic rules, highways would become demolition derbies. Without community laws, we'd be living in war zones. Everything and everybody needs rules. Dog trainers, the military, video games, contests—and UFG. I was barely into my fitness program before I realized I had to set up some tough nonnegotiable rules for exercise, diet, and general health. If you're committed to following a similar plan, you'll need rules, too.

To play UFG, you'll need two levels of rules. You'll need minimum and optimal rules. For instance, you may decide that three days of exercise each week is the nonnegotiable minimum, but five is the optimal rule you're striving for—the ultimate goal. If you know for sure that you'll have a busy end of the week, you may not be able to get in five workouts, but you know you must find time in the first part of the week for at least three workouts. The at-least-three-preferably-five rule keeps you from skipping so many workouts early in the week that you can't follow your rule.

You'll need two levels of rules for eating, too. By now you should have calculated the number of calories you need to maintain your weight on an average day. That number should be your minimum, nonnegotiable rule. Tell yourself that under no circumstances can you have more than the number of calories you need to maintain your weight. Now set a reasonable number of calories less than the number you need to maintain your weight. That number can be the optimal calorie intake you're striving for—the ultimate goal that leads to weight *loss*.

For instance, if you need 3,000 calories to maintain your body weight, you can't have more than 3,000 calories, no matter what. If your ultimate goal is 2,500 calories and you reach that goal for a week, you'll lose 1 pound (500 calories x 7 days = 3,500, the number of calories that make you gain or lose a pound). And if your ultimate goal is 2,000 calories a day, you'll lose 2 pounds a week if you meet that goal.

Here are some other rules I follow:

No wasted calories until I've covered all my nutritional needs.

My goal is total fitness, and I have to be sure I spend my calories on foods that will keep me healthy and give me energy for my workouts. It's never an option to substitute a cookie for a serving of lean meat. If I want a treat, I have to purchase it with "money" left over after buying all the fuel I need for the day. Too many kids are overfed and undernourished. I know because I was once one of them.

Absolutely no trans fat.

That's my unbendable rule. Trans fats are terrible for you. They were created to give foods a longer shelf life, but they can quickly reduce the life of the person who consumes them. Trans fats are made from safe unsaturated liquid oils, but the process of turning them to solid changes their properties to dangerous. They're used in margarine and in most packaged cakes, chips, and cookies. Most of the time, chicken, fish, and French fries are fried in solid vegetable shortening that contains trans fats.

Trans fats have been called the biggest food disaster in history, and it's easy to see why. Now that we've consumed foods with trans fats for a couple of decades, we know that they promote heart disease, cancer, diabetes, immune and reproductive system problems, and obesity. My goal is total fitness, not just a thin body, so my "no trans fats" rule is actually just common sense. I check the ingredients on the package and turn down even one potato chip with trans fat. You can find baked potato chips, so I hold out for them.

No food after supper.

No exceptions. If I have calories left to spend, I spend them at supper. Eating late would be an easy habit to get into, and I can't afford it. This rule may not work for you, especially if you eat supper early or go to bed late. If your time between supper and lights out is long, how about setting a calorie limit for evening snacking instead of cutting it out altogether? For instance, your rule could be "After supper, eat no more than 200 calories and be sure they come from healthy snacks."

Never eat directly from a bag, jar, box, or package.

It's too easy to overeat without realizing it. If I want a snack from a family-size container, I check the nutritional panel for the serving size. I transfer a serving size to a bowl or napkin before digging in. When that's gone, I don't go back for seconds.

If I'm hungry after eating, I wait 15 minutes to see if the feeling goes away.

Usually it does. My stomach is already full. It's just that my brain hasn't gotten the message yet. If I wait 15 minutes, I'm usually no longer hungry. If I am, I listen to my body and grab a healthy snack.

Never use food to fight stress, keep me company, or entertain me.

Food is fuel. Exercise combats stress. Friends and family keep you company. Movies and video games entertain. When I'm faced with stress, loneliness, or boredom, I remind myself of the right ways to deal with whatever I'm facing.

Count every calorie that goes into my mouth, no matter how small.

Whatever, whenever eating got me into size-44 jeans. I stay on guard against mindless eating by counting every calorie and rounding up if I'm unsure of the serving size.

Don't mix one day's calories with the next.

I don't borrow calories from tomorrow to make up for today's overeating. Every day is a new screen in **UFG**. I start off with a new amount of "money" to spend. Saving up calories or borrowing from the next day gets too complicated. You're sure to end up eating too much when you try to deal with more than one day at a time.

Never go below 1,400 calories in a day.

Once the DSL generation decides to get fit, most of us want to lose weight at lightning speed. The idea is to get healthy and fit, not to starve your body of the nutrients it needs to operate. That's the quickest way to kill a fitness plan. No one can operate for long without enough fuel. I can't work out, handle school activities, and hang out with friends on a handful of Cheerios and a diet drink any more than I could drive a car from Atlanta to LA on a half tank of gas. Most health experts warn adults not to go below 1,200 calories a day, but I set 1,400 as my personal standard since teens need more calories. And I'd never keep my calories that low for more than a day or two. Fourteen hundred is just the bare minimum, the line I don't let myself cross.

Exercise no less than three times a week.

No exceptions.

Include cardio and strength training in every workout.

To reach all my health and fitness goals, I make this a personal rule. Some people alternate cardio and strength training, but including both at every workout sessions works for me.

Never use pills, muscle-enhancement supplements, or any other dangerous shortcuts.
A good rule is "If you would hesitate to tell your parents or doctor that you're taking something, don't take it." Quick fixes are tempting when you have a lot of weight to lose. They may work for a while, but when you stop using them—which you're almost certain to do—you haven't developed a lifetime fitness plan, so you'll likely gain back all the weight you struggled to lose. And while you're looking for a quick fix, you could easily cause permanent damage to the body you're trying so hard to repair. Pills and supplements are dangerous, and they have no place in **UFG**.

If you want to get serious about your rules, put them in writing or share them with someone you trust and who's supportive of your fitness program. And every week or two go over your rules and make sure you're obeying them. Holding yourself accountable to your rules will lessen the chance that you'll blur the lines and let your fitness program start slipping.

Some of my rules may work for you, but you're going to need your own rules, too. Pull out your journal or open your computer file. Make your own list of rules and consider them your strategy guide in **UFG**.

MAKING FRIENDS WITH THE ENEMY

Sometimes I think it would be easier if I cut out eating altogether. No more choices. No more measuring. No more temptations. The new rule would just be "no more food." Unfortunately, it can't work that way. It's eat or die, so every day is filled with choices. The wrong foods in the wrong quantities make food your enemy. But since you need food for fuel, you have to make friends with the enemy.

It's harder when you're a kid because most general food choices are out of your control. Even if you want to cook something yourself, you have to depend on others to help you. You have to request special ingredients, and you usually have to ask someone else to buy them. If you can't cook, you're in even worse shape. And if your family goes out to eat, you're probably not the one who chooses the restaurant.

In spite of these limitations, you can do a lot to eat healthy. Start by making little changes in all of your meals, regardless of who's cooking or where you're eating. You'll be amazed at how quickly saved calories translate into lost pounds.

Here are some general things you can do.

Eat your foods as plain as possible.

I've found that it's the sneaky little extras that can make the difference in success and failure. I can eat a lot more healthy food by not wasting my calorie "money" on extras like condiments, butter, cream sauces, and gravies. You'll miss them at first, but after a while, foods will taste better without them.

Bread is delicious. Unfortunately, most of us have turned it into a holder for other goodies, and we don't notice the taste. Try eating a sandwich of just meat and whole-grain bread—no condiments or toppings—and notice how great the bread tastes. Now that I appreciate bread, I sometimes grab a plain piece for a quick snack.

If the food you're served is hidden under gravies and sauces, you can save hundreds of calories by just scraping off the toppings. If the chicken that's put on your plate is fried in the skin, peel off the skin and the breaded coating and enjoy the meat. You can save 220 calories on a chicken breast and 130 on a drumstick by getting rid of the coating and skin. And if you choose white chicken meat over dark meat, you'll save a bundle, too. A big meaty chicken breast is 140 calories (without skin and breading) and a leg and thigh is 290.

Get rid of all visible fat.

If you see grease floating on anything, wipe it off or spoon it out. Drain hamburgers, even if you just blot them with a napkin or paper towel. Just 1 tablespoon of grease is 100 calories. Cut the fat off steak and pot roast and save 250 calories for every ounce you remove.

Know and measure portions.

When food is served family style, it's easy to serve yourself too much. Know portion sizes, even for starchy vegetables like peas and corn. Veggies are good for you, but an extra half-cup serving of corn is 65–95 calories and an extra half-cup of peas is 60.

Here are some general guidelines on portion sizes:

Vegetables: ½ to ¾ cup. Measure out a half-cup of a vegetable to get an idea of what a serving looks like. Now pour the serving onto a plate so you can recognize a vegetable serving.

Cereal: ½ to 1 cup, depending on the type of cereal. A serving of a heavier granola cereal is usually ½ cup; a serving of a flake cereal can be as much as a cup. Measure a serving of cereal and find a small bowl or cup that barely fits the serving. Use it each time you have cereal and you won't be able to overload the bowl.

Meat: 3 ounces. A serving of meat should fit into the palm of your hand with room to spare.

Fruit: 1 apple, orange, or pear. One small banana or half of a large one. Six strawberries or fifteen grapes. A half-cup of diced or canned fruit (choose "packed in its own juice" and save a wad of "money").

Cake: ½₂ of a 9-inch cake

Pie: ⅙ to ⅛ of an 8-inch pie (UFG does *not* include cakes and pies. I just wanted to show you how small a "real" serving is so if you decide to "buy" one, you'll cut an accurate slice.)

Be aware when eating out.

Almost all restaurants publish their menus and nutritional information online, even fast-food restaurants. Check out the restaurants your family likes and find the healthiest foods on the menu. You may be surprised that some foods that sound healthy are not the best choices.

Before we eat out, I usually check the restaurant website and have an idea of what I want to order. If that's not possible, I order the plainest beef, fish, or chicken on the menu, along with steamed vegetables. Some restaurants have a portion of their menu marked "heart healthy," and they supply calorie, protein, and carb counts. I choose from those entrees if they're available. I always ask to substitute steamed veggies for fries, and I ask for low-cal salad dressing on the side.

Restaurants try to compete by offering generous portions, but don't be misled into thinking their portions are official serving sizes. If restaurant portions are supersized, ask your server for a to-go box and put all but one serving of each food into the box *before* you start eating. You'll probably have enough leftovers for another full meal.

The better prepared you are when you go to a restaurant, the healthier you'll eat. But if you find yourself in a restaurant with no warning and no nutritional information available, do your homework when you get home. Determine how many calories you consumed and add them to your day's quota. And if you know in the morning that you'll be eating in a new restaurant that evening, save a few calories from each meal and snack so you'll have some extra calories to spend at supper.

"Eating out" can also include parties and just hanging out with friends. Most snacks at teen parties center around hot dogs, soft drinks, chips, and dips. And once you start to nibble, it's hard to stop and nearly impossible to keep up with the calories.

I don't stop playing UFG just because I'm hanging out with friends. I remind myself that the real fun of a party is friends, not food. As long as I have a bottle of water or a Coke Zero in my hand, I forget about the stacks of snacks.

If friends come to my house, Mom tries to have a variety of snacks, including healthy ones. But since there's no way to know what foods you'll find at someone else's house, I eat something healthy before I leave home and then concentrate on the party. If I find a platter of carrot and celery sticks, or a basket of granola bars, I consider it a bonus—but I don't plan on it.

Be smart when eating in.

When your family spreads a home-cooked meal on the table, are you more likely to see salads and grilled steaks or pasta, Italian bread presoaked with garlic butter, and giant wedges of chocolate cake? Of course, your job is easier if your family is already eating healthy, but you can eat smart regardless.

If less-than-healthy, high-calorie foods are your choices, remove sauces, gravies, toppings, and condiments. Drain grease. Get rid of all visible fat. Remove the skin and breading from chicken. Cut portion sizes. (Am I sounding redundant? Good! Because these are major strategies of UFG.)

That's how I operated for the first months of my fitness program, when I was keeping my plan to myself. Not too many people noticed, and those who did just thought I was a little quirky about what I ate. The only comment I received was to please stop wiping gravy on my grandmother's linen napkins. After a few grease-stained napkins, she started giving me paper towels to scrape my meats.

The turning point in family meals was when I became more open about my fitness goals. My family jumped in to help. The cooks in the family now make sure every meal has foods I can eat. They've revised some of the family recipes to reduce calories and make meals healthier. Visit www.cuttingmyselfinhalf.com for some of their recipes. Maybe the cooks in your family will try them. Most are easy enough for you to make yourself (or so I hear).

Learn to fend for yourself.

To me, cooking usually means microwaving a frozen dinner or serving up cereal, but sometimes I get adventurous and make a sandwich or make my own salad (usually with the help of a restaurant salad bar).

When I'm fixing myself a sandwich or a salad, I try to cut calories every way I can while making my meal as healthy as possible. Here's an example of two ways to make a ham sandwich— one friend and one foe.

Sandwich 1

2 slices of white bread,
180 calories

2 slices (total 4 oz.) regular ham,
120 calories

2 slices of Swiss cheese,
120 calories

2 tablespoons of regular mayonnaise,
200 calories

3 leaves lettuce,
3 calories

2 tomato slices,
6 calories

Total calories: 629

Sandwich 2

2 slices reduced-calorie wheat bread,
90 calories

6 slices extra lean deli-thin ham,
60 calories

3 leaves of lettuce,
3 calories

2 tomato slices,
6 calories

Total calories: 159

See how easy it is to save 470 calories? If you make just these few changes on a sandwich you eat each day, you could lose nearly a pound a week. Changes like these are some of the easiest ways to reduce calories—you still consume the same things in the same quantities, just low-calorie versions without some of the frills. Once you get used to a dressed-down sandwich you'll learn to enjoy the tastes of bread and meat. They're delicious by themselves.

Salads can also be healthy or dangerous. Lots of people who want to lose weight decide to have salads every day, thinking they're low-cal. They can be, of course, but they can also be higher in calories than a burger and fries. If you're ordering a salad in a restaurant, you can order it minus bacon, cheese, and other high-calorie ingredients. Choose a salad with grilled chicken instead of fried and save more than 100 calories.

Here's an example of two salads—one friend and one foe.

Salad 1

3 cups shredded iceberg lettuce,
30 calories
3 ounces fried chicken,
210 calories
¼ cup shredded blue cheese,
120 calories
3 slices bacon, crumbled,
150 calories
¼ sugared pecans,
120 calories
½ cup croutons,
65 calories
1/3 cup dried, sweetened cranberries,
140 calories
4 tablespoons Thousand Island
dressing,
360 calories
Total calories: 1,195

Salad 2

3 cups shredded iceberg lettuce,
30 calories
3 ounces grilled chicken,
140 calories
¼ cup sliced strawberries,
15 calories
¼ cup grated carrots,
12 calories
3½ low-fat Triscuits, broken,
60 calories
2 tbsp fat-free ranch dressing
50 calories
Total calories: 307

Another big savings: 888 calories, which translates into a fourth of a pound. See how you can cut calories without cutting volume? I eat six meals and snacks every day, and I'm rarely hungry. One of the major ways I cut calories is by making good food choices and removing the hidden calories. And since I don't starve myself, I can stick to my new lifestyle more easily.

You can reduce calories a lot of other ways while hardly noticing the difference. Almost any recipe can use fat-free milk, cream cheese, or sour cream instead of the regular versions. Splenda or Splenda Sugar Blend can replace sugar. Egg whites or Egg Beaters can replace whole eggs. Now that I've discovered healthy, low-calorie Egg Beaters, I have eggs for breakfast a couple of times a week.

Exchange empty calories for energy and nutrition.

In **UFG**, the calories you save can add up to lost pounds or you can use some of them to fuel your body for exercise. Here are some examples of how exchanging empty calories for energy and nutrition can make a difference in just one day.

For breakfast, reduce your usual one cup of granola and one cup of whole milk to half a cup of granola and half a cup of fat-free milk. You'll save 220 calories, enough to "buy" a basic turkey sandwich with low-calorie whole-grain bread. Exchange a packaged honey bun for an apple and save 275 calories, which can be turned into fruit snacks throughout the day: a banana, a pear, and an orange.

At lunch, drain a tablespoon of grease from your hamburger and save 100 calories, enough to add ¾ cup of steamed broccoli to your meal. Instead of chili cheese fries, have a cup of steamed broccoli and save 650 calories, enough for two healthy frozen dinners. Talk about adding two filling, fantastic snacks to your day! Or you could have one frozen dinner for a pre-exercise snack and squirrel the rest of the calories away for weight loss.

For supper, have grilled chicken instead of country fried steak with gravy and save 400 calories. That's enough for a six-inch turkey sub, an apple, and an 8-ounce glass of fat-free milk. Have a baked potato with 3 tablespoons of salsa instead of 2 tablespoons each of butter and sour cream, ¼ cup of grated cheese, and one slice of bacon. The calories saved—420—could "buy" a 5½-ounce sirloin steak. Enjoy the bread, but without 2 tablespoons of butter, and save 200 calories. Have a granola bar with the calories saved.

Throughout the day, replace two regular soft drinks with diet drinks or water. Save 280 calories. Use them to "buy" 5 ounces of roasted white meat chicken. Choose fat-free milk instead of whole milk and save 110 calories on two 8-ounce glasses per day. A hundred calories can "buy" a banana.

With just these changes, you can easily save enough calories to cover three snacks and keep your body evenly fueled throughout the day. See how quickly hidden calories add up and how easily you can cut frills and actually eat more filling foods?

The **UFG** strategies I've talked about are like the difference between walking across a college campus and getting a degree. If you just want to say you've been to college, take a walk. If you want to change your future, get a degree. If you want to play at losing weight, make a few attempts at cutting back. If you want to win **UFG**, set goals and deadlines, enlist support, make rules and stick to them, and change your relationship with food.

10

Your 24/7 Coach

It's great to have friends and family who will support your new lifestyle. It's nice to live in the tech age where you can find global support with just a few clicks of the mouse. But no support system is available 24/7 except self-talk. So as you play the ULTIMATE FITNESS GAME (UFG), be sure you have an imaginary sound card filled with self-coaching ideas, thoughts, and phrases—things you've internalized and can pull from your memory the very second someone offers you a cookie or you're tempted to skip your workout.

By self-talk, I mean images and reminders—both positive and negative—that you can pull from your memory when you're tempted to take a step backward in your fitness program. I'm fortunate to have a great family/friends/school support system, but ultimately, *I'm* responsible for *my* fitness. It's up to me to serve as my own coach during the many times when it's me alone facing a plate of cookies. I use self-coaching to get on track and stay on track.

WHAT YOUR IMAGINATION CAN DO FOR YOU

When I started my plan and had more than 100 pounds to lose, my favorite self-coaching technique was imagining a meeting with someone I rarely saw, usually a friend or a cousin. I'd imagine them knocking on my door a year from now. I'd open the door and see their astonished face when they saw a thin, healthy Taylor LeBaron. That scenario kept me going to the YMCA and gave me the strength to pass up plenty of unhealthy snacks.

I was able to live that scenario several times after losing weight. By the time I reached my ideal weight, I was attending Chrysalis (best school on the planet), but I still had friends at my old school. Sometimes I'd run into old friends, and it was fun seeing their shocked faces. Some didn't recognize me—I had to tell them who I was.

Some kids found my Facebook page and e-mailed to say they couldn't believe the change. Whenever I got that sort of reaction, I'd remember the times I had self-coached myself with the same scenario. It was doubly fun when I realized my self-coaching was a dream come true.

Store up at least one scenario that you can pull out when you need it. Here are some ideas to get you started.

→ Imagine overhearing someone calling you skinny. Imagine how you'll feel when you hear those words. Imagine how you'll look and act when you hear them. You'll be thin. Your shirt will be tucked in, and it will hang loosely. Your jeans will be slim fit. You'll walk with confidence. Your movements will be quick and smooth and light. You'll ease into the chair no one else wants because it's so small. Then you'll hear someone say, "Good, the skinniest person took the tiny chair."

↬ Imagine that you're supposed to meet someone at a restaurant, someone you've never seen before. A friend calls to describe you to the person, and you hear your friend use the word "thin" or "slim." Again, don't just think of the scenario. Imagine how you look and act. Imagine how you feel when you hear yourself described as thin. And know that someday you'll live this dream-come-true.

↬ Imagine being interviewed for a major magazine about your 100-pound weight loss. The reporter says that readers are eager to learn about your weight-loss method because it's been so effective for you. Readers want to know your secret to a healthy, fit body.

↬ Imagine appearing on a major TV talk show. They show a "before" picture of you. Then you walk onstage—slim and energetic—and the audience applauds. It's happened to me, and it can happen to you. Start imagining it now.

↬ Imagine yourself 100 pounds lighter and wearing your biggest jeans. They're so big that both your legs fit into one pants leg. You can stretch the waist so far in front that you could add a pillow.

↬ Imagine that you spend the day at a friend's house, someone you always considered skinny. The weather changes, and your friend offers to loan you a sweater. Imagine slipping it over your head and feeling how large it is on you. You push up the sleeves, and pull the bottom of the sweater up to keep it from sagging. Imagine the rush of feeling that too-big sweater.

↬ Imagine running effortlessly, winning a race at school. Let yourself experience how it feels to be the first one over the finish line.

NEGATIVE MEMORIES CAN SERVE A PURPOSE

Another way I coach myself is through negative memories. It's sort of like the time, when I was three, when I took the bulb out of the lamp in my room and pressed my finger as far into the socket as I could. I got a big enough jolt of electricity to teach me to stay away from light sockets. Negative self-coaching isn't very pleasant, but when all else fails in UFG, I use it.

Like most formerly fat people, I have plenty of embarrassing moments I can use for negative coaching. One of my "favorite" negative self-coaching memories is the time I tried to imitate Bo Duke and got stuck halfway-in/halfway-out of Mom's car window. I still cringe when I remember that, and it's enough to get me running to the gym.

Put a couple of your worst fat memories on your imaginary DVD and pull them up when you're tempted to choose the wrong foods, overeat, or underexercise. Here are a couple of ideas to get you started:

→ Recall your most embarrassing moment associated with being overweight. Did another kid make fun of you in front of someone you had a crush on? Did a relative insist you try on a sweater they bought you for your birthday, right away, in front of everyone—and it was too small? Did you break a chair at a friend's house? How did you feel? What did you do or say? Remember as many details of the incident as possible, and bring it to your memory as vividly as you can. Relive it, and promise yourself that nothing like it will ever happen again.

→ Remember the worst fat joke made at your expense. Maybe a family member or friend said something they thought was hilarious. You laughed, along with everyone else, but you were actually humiliated. When things like that happened to me, I experienced physical reactions like flushing and trembling. If you experience physical reactions to embarrassment about your weight, remember these reactions when you're tempted to give up on fitness.

→ Remember the worst thing said by someone that was meant to be hateful. It wasn't a joke. It was deliberately meant to hurt. Some people are just mean, and some people honestly don't like fat people. Most of us have heard at least one person say something deliberately hateful. Pull up your worst memory and use it to make sure no one can ever say anything like that about you again.

→ Recall a time when you overate to the point where something delicious no longer tasted good. In fact, it tasted sickening, and you were disgusted with yourself for eating it. Imagine that's how you'll feel if you eat a food that's tempting you.

→ Think of a time when you overheard someone talking about your size, when they didn't know you were listening. Maybe your parents were talking about how concerned they were about your weight. Maybe you heard some teachers talking. Or the nurses at your doctor's office. Or someone in a department store or restaurant. Part of you probably wanted to walk right up to whoever was talking and tell them how rude and cruel they were being. But you probably just listened and hurt on the inside. Remember that hurt and use the memory to be sure it doesn't happen again.

→ What's the worst memory you have of being weighed? I can still recall the nurses at Dr. Bagheri's office going on and on about my weight. Is your worst weigh-in memory set at the doctor's office? Did it occur at school? At home? Remember the worst time, how it felt, how you reacted. Use the memory to your advantage to make sure this time next year you love stepping on a scale.

→ Remember how discouraged you are as you eat the last bite of a bad-choice snack. It never tastes as good as the first bite because once you're stuffed, you're disgusted with yourself for letting a craving control you. Feel that feeling before you make the choice instead of afterward. Live what the last bite will taste like.

POP-UP PEP TALKS
Are *You* Talkin' to *Me*?

Once I got close to my ideal weight, I found that the quickest, most effective coachings were short reminders that flashed through my mind in seconds. I can give myself an instant pep talk, even while I'm talking with friends. I use instant pep talks all the time, almost unconsciously. It takes only a few seconds to tell myself:

→ You've worked too hard to blow it all on a couple of potato chips.

→ It feels great to slip on these 30-waist jeans. Do you really want to go back to a 32?

→ That cookie will taste good for a few seconds, but as

soon as you realize you've blown all those calories, it won't taste so good.

→ Being thin feels better than any food could taste.

→ Are you really hungry, or are you just wanting to taste this cake? Food is fuel; wait till you're hungry to eat.

→ Why are you reaching for seconds? If you're lonely, call a friend. If you're bored, watch a movie. If you're stressed, exercise. If you're honestly hungry, wait 15 minutes. If you're still hungry, eat just enough of something healthy to take away your hungry feeling.

→ How will you feel 30 minutes after eating this?

→ You can wait till supper. It's only 30 more minutes.

→ If you eat another sandwich you'll have to run 30 minutes longer on the treadmill just to "pay" for it.

→ You deserve to be thin!

→ You're wearing a disguise, and it's about time you showed people the amazing person you really are. You can't do that unless you get fit.

→ One day at a time. You only have to worry about this choice, right now, right this minute. Your goal is to resist just this one temptation.

Any of these pep talks can work for you, too, and you can probably think of plenty of others. The key is to memorize them so you can pull them up fast when you need them.

ROLE MODELS AS INSPIRATION

Sometimes in UFG, I use role models and their positive qualities to self-coach myself to be more like them. Of course, John Schneider has been a role model for a long time. He's thin, agile, and full of energy. He's dedicated to fitness, and he's the same size now as when he played Bo Duke in 1978. Those are all qualities I admire, so John Schneider inspires me to have the same qualities. I coach myself to remove obstacles that keep me from being as thin, agile, and energetic as possible. I tell myself that if John Schneider can remain trim for thirty years, I can, too.

Another role model is Walter Keeping. He was my teacher at my old school, when my weight was at its highest, and I always admired his outdoor, athletic abilities. Walter grew up in Canada, and he loves the out-of-doors, camping, and hiking—all the

It's Never Too Late

Self-coaching can even work when you've already taken a big bite of a food you promised yourself you wouldn't eat. If you find yourself with a mouthful of pie, you can stop after that first bite. Savor the bite—the first bite is always the most delicious, anyway. After you've experienced the taste, ask yourself:

Will the second bite taste better or not quite as good?

Would I rather enjoy the rest of this food for two or three more minutes or spend hours feeling great because I resisted the temptation to eat the rest?

things I found difficult to do when I weighed nearly 300 pounds. But Walter always encouraged me and assumed the best about me. This year, when school started, there was Walter—a teacher at my new school! It was fun to meet him again after two years and tell him that when I hiked up Amicalola Falls with kids from Chrysalis he was one of my inspirations.

I definitely have people I look up to and want to be like— from my favorite actor to an unforgettable teacher to my grandfather and my mother. But my best inspiration is realizing my own potential. I know I was created unique and amazing. I may never be the absolute best at anything, but I know I have huge potential that I haven't yet reached.

When I think of the possibilities and opportunities for my future, I want to clear away all the obstacles to being the best *I* can be. I know that extra weight caused people to react to me in a different way, and it limited the careers I could consider. My own potential inspires me to be fit, slim, and healthy.

Who are your role models? It's nice to have people to look up to and want to be like. But it's most important to like yourself enough to do your personal best at everything you do.

WHOA! DID YOU KNOW?

If you've been telling yourself, like I did, that you're just a big kid and your weight doesn't get in the way of accomplishing your life goals, here are some things to think about, some facts to keep in mind when you're self-coaching:

→ People say that you're more likely to be hired for a great job if you're thin. That's lousy but true. Most people don't take time to look on the inside to see the remarkable individual you are. Some people associate extra pounds with laziness and poor work performance. Ouch! Talk about unfair labels.

→ People are nicer to you when you're thin—another rotten thing that just shouldn't be but is. You've probably seen TV shows where some thin guy or girl gets dressed up in padded clothes and pretends to need help. The guy may ask for directions or the girl may ask for help carrying a package 20 feet to a post office. While they're dressed in the fat suit, most people ignore them.

Then, the next day, these same people ask for the same help in the same place—but without the extra pounds. People are only too glad to help.

Let's face it. People go for the wrapper It's not fair, but it's a fact of life and we have to live with it. Overweight kids live in a world that loves thin people. We probably can't do a lot to change that.

→ Everybody loves a good joke, but not when they're the punch line. If you're carrying extra pounds, I'll bet you've been the brunt of plenty of jokes, even from friends. You probably pretended to laugh with the jokester, but has all that hammering at your ego finally put cracks in your self-esteem?

→ When you're obese, your weight sometimes determines your friends. Not the hobbies and interests you share. Not the type of music you enjoy. Not the movies you see. Often, thin kids don't want to hang out with fat kids, so you find other overweight kids to be your friends. And all that you have in common are the problems we've just mentioned.

- Overweight people are more likely to develop several types of cancer. Life is fun, and who wants to up their chances of cutting it short?
- Excess weight makes your heart work harder. If you wear yours out too soon, you'll face all sorts of heart-related problems in adulthood.
- Kids can get type 2 diabetes. That's the type you normally develop later in life. It used to be rare for kids to develop type 2 diabetes, but today it's more and more common. And if you continue your overweight lifestyle, diabetes is almost certain to be in your adult future. Diabetes can slow you down and get in the way of living the incredible life you deserve to live.
- You have less energy when you carry extra pounds. More weight, less energy. Less weight, more energy. It's that simple.
- If you're an obese teen, you're just as likely not to make it to old age as a teen who's a heavy smoker. Maybe they should put a Surgeon General's warning on chili cheese fries.
- Sometimes kids can't wait to grow up, but who wants adult diseases before you get your driver's license? Today, in addition to type 2 diabetes, more and more kids are being diagnosed with arthritis and asthma, plus high blood pressure and high cholesterol, which lead to heart disease. Fat can accumulate in a kid's arteries just like an adult's. Fat in the arteries blocks circulation. Your heart has to pump with more force, which gears you up for—yikes—a heart attack.
- Obesity slows you down. I know from experience how

easy it was to get winded just walking up my driveway. Doing all the things kids are supposed to do—riding bikes, playing baseball, running races, playing tag—aren't options when your heart is pounding and your thighs are rubbing till they're raw. The bigger you get, the less likely you'll exercise. And the less you exercise, the bigger you'll get. It's like being caught in a maze with no way out.

→ Kids in the United States are carrying too much weight. The Centers for Disease Control and Prevention says that the percentage of overweight kids has doubled since 1980. And get this: The number of overweight teens has tripled. That's a 300 percent increase.

→ Worldwide statistics are scary, too. So many kids—and adults—are putting on so many extra pounds that the World Health Organization has created an international task force to figure out what's happening and how to control our super size. Would you believe that, worldwide, 300 million people are obese and 750 million—that's three-quarters of a billion—are overweight? That's one-eighth of the world's population. But don't get comfortable thinking you're just part of a new trend and soon fat will be popular. Extra pounds come with extra problems. Social. Emotional. Occupational. Physical. Sixty percent of overweight kids *already* have at least one risk factor for heart disease.

Some of these facts are pretty scary. But don't get scared. Get fit. I did, and you can, too. Now, here are some more facts that aren't scary. They can actually inspire you, so be sure to keep this information in mind when you self-coach.

↪ Little changes mount up. Lose the 2 tablespoons of mayonnaise on just one sandwich a day, and you'll lose 20 pounds in a year (as long as you don't add the calories somewhere else in your diet). Assuming you have 3 cups of milk each day in cereal or as a drink, switching to fat-free milk will lower your weight by 22 pounds a year.

↪ Exercise whittles away the calories, but it also makes you smaller in actual size than someone who weighs the same. A toned, muscular body is smaller than a body with a large percentage of extra fat.

↪ Walking just 20 minutes a day at 3 mph will burn 133 calories if you weigh 250 (106 if you weigh 200, 80 if you weigh 150), creating a weight loss of nearly 14 pounds in a year (11 pounds if you're 200 pounds and 8 pounds if you're 150), but making you appear that you've lost much more and improving your health immeasurably.

↪ Regular exercise increases your metabolism, which means that your body makes better use of the calories you consume. More exercise = better calorie burning = more weight loss.

↪ People who exercise have more energy. Weird as it seems, try exercising when you're tired and you'll be amazed at the energy you feel.

↪ Your bones get stronger when you eat well and exercise.

↪ Your skin gets healthier when you eat well and exercise. Most teens worry about acne, and diet and exercise may help as much as expensive ointments.

And here is the *most* important fact to remember as you play **UFG**:

→ The only way to lose weight and keep it off is to value who you are right now and to *know* that you deserve to be thin. Then make fitness a lifestyle, and you'll only have to lose weight once. Lose the weight once—because you deserve to be thin—and never worry about being overweight again. Do that by making fitness your lifestyle, not a temporary diet.

Conclusion

FROM FAT TO FIT

You can be the person who moves from fat to fit.
How do I know? If I could do it, so can you. Try this. Imagine your ultimate dream life—what you would be and do if you had no limitations. Imagine how great it would be. Now think of all the things that keep you from being the person you dream of being. I don't know your situation, and I don't know what your limitations are. Some barriers to your future may be tougher than I can imagine. But there's one barrier that's movable. If you're overweight, you can move that boulder to the side and then smash it into a million tiny pieces. You *can* get rid of the weight.

You may have what it takes to be whatever you want to be. But are your skills and personality and confidence hiding behind layers of fat? Push obesity aside and step forward as a lean, fit, and confident person. Start thinking of yourself as built tough, bursting with energy, and optimistic about the future. See yourself as a thin, successful adult—maybe the CEO of a company, interviewed regularly on TV. Imagine your future family photo.

There you are in the middle, surrounded by your spouse and kids. You look great—healthy, lean, and well dressed!

If you're serious about facing your fitness challenge, you'll need to create a program that works for you. My program—the ULTIMATE FITNESS GAME—works for me, and I think a lot of it will fit your needs. But take what works for you and leave the rest. Build your personal fitness program, but whatever program you build, be sure it includes these UFG rules.

→ Don't starve—eat at least 1,400 calories a day.

→ Eat healthy. Your goals are getting healthy and getting thin (in that order). Spending your reduced calories on unhealthy foods doesn't make long-term sense.

→ Think of food as fuel—not companionship, entertainment, or a stress buster.

→ Exercise. It not only promotes weight loss; it also promotes good health, relieves stress, and even reduces depression.

→ Start out slowly in all aspects of your fitness plan, increasing exercise and reducing calories a little at a time. If you do too much too fast, you'll burn out before you've burned the calories you need to be thin.

→ Count. Measure. Keep track. Document. That's the safest way to face the facts and deal with them.

I hope these ideas help. Getting fit has been one of my biggest accomplishments, but I'll consider it multiplied if others can learn from it. Good luck! E-mail me at taylor@cuttingmy selfinhalf.com to tell me your success story. I know I'll hear from you soon!

Afterword

When I weighed nearly 300 pounds, I had only one goal: get rid of the weight. I soon realized that losing weight would do more for me than just get me into smaller jeans. Fitness became a springboard for achieving other life goals. As my weight dropped, my opportunities rose. It seemed as if new doors opened for me every day.

All my life, I'd been an incredible person—just like you are an incredible person *right now*—but few people noticed until I got rid of the extra pounds. In the summer before my junior year of high school, I received a powerful reminder of how playing the ULTIMATE FITNESS GAME had opened doors to new opportunities. One June morning, I awoke to the tune of my cell phone. The lady on the phone congratulated me and said I'd been chosen to carry the Olympic torch for the 2010 Winter Olympics in Canada. Still groggy, I let the news sink in. I would be one of ten teens representing Coca-Cola, and I'd been nominated because I "exemplified positive living." Nominees were judged on involvement in community service, concern for the environment—and physical fitness.

As I thought about why I'd been selected from so many qualified teens, I realized that fitness opened a door that otherwise would have been closed to me. Even if fitness hadn't been one of the criteria for selection, I doubt I would have been nominated if I were twice my current size.

I thought about what it meant to carry the Olympic torch, a tradition that began in 1936. The torch would be carried from Olympia, Greece, to Calgary, Canada, by boat, airplane, camel, dogsled, and people like me. But at the time I was carrying the torch, I'd be the only person in a world of 6.7 billion people who was entrusted with the Olympic flame. During my assigned time, I would be fully responsible for getting the flame to its destination. That early morning phone call announced one of the greatest honors in my life—*so far*.

I know the Olympics is just the beginning. Fitness will open many doors in my lifetime because now people can see the *amazingly amazing* Taylor LeBaron who's been there all the time. I know you're amazing, too, because everyone is phenomenal in some way. I hope you'll join me in the ULTIMATE FITNESS GAME and prove to the whole world just how amazing you are.

You may have picked up this book thinking, *I want to lose weight*. That's a start, but "lose weight" is a pretty weak goal. Most people can do that, even if just for a short time. But some people use unhealthy methods to take off pounds fast, leaving their bodies in worse shape than people in Third World countries. I hope your goal, like mine, is a lifetime of fitness.

Don't settle for less. If being fit is worth achieving, it's a big enough deal to make a clear plan and do it right. I know you will, so I'll sign off with GJP—good job, partner!

Appendix

SMART SUBSTITUTIONS & REDUCTIONS

You could call me a food fan, a connoisseur of most things delicious. I love the tastes, smells, and textures of a variety of foods. I view food as fuel for my body, but it doesn't mean I can't enjoy the process of fueling up. My love for food didn't go away when I began playing the ULTIMATE FITNESS GAME (UFG). I still look forward to a great meal. But I like to think that I've refined my love for food—sort of raised the bar to a new level. Now I appreciate food without all the unhealthy bows and wrappings. Our busy family depends a lot on healthy frozen dinners and nutritious prepackaged snacks, but my mom and grandmother make sure I get plenty of home-cooked foods, as well.

One great advantage to home-cooked meals is that you can make adjustments that cut calories without cutting taste. Almost any recipe can be made healthier with a few substitutions and reductions.

Here are some changes that have little or no effect on taste:

→ Use fat-free dairy products, such as cottage cheese, sour cream, and milk, instead of the whole-fat versions. Doing this can save you a lot of calories. Take a look:

Not-So-Good	Better	Best
1 ounce regular cottage cheese, 120 calories	1 ounce reduced-fat cottage cheese, 25 calories	1 ounce fat-free cottage cheese, 20 calories
1 ounce regular sour cream, 60 calories	1 ounce reduced-fat sour cream, 50 calories	1 ounce fat-free sour cream, 20 calories
1 cup whole milk, 150 calories	1 cup 2% milk, 120 calories	1 cup fat-free milk, 85 calories
1 ounce regular cheddar cheese, 115 calories	1 ounce reduced-fat cheddar cheese, 80 calories	1 ounce fat-free cheddar cheese, 50 calories
1 tablespoon regular butter, 100 calories	1 tablespoon light butter, 75 calories	1 tablespoon reduced-calorie vegetable oil and butter (with no trans fat), 60 calories
1 ounce regular cream cheese, 100 calories	1 ounce reduced-fat cream cheese, 60 calories	1 ounce fat-free cream cheese, 30 calories

→ Use less butter than a recipe calls for. Chances are, you won't notice, and you'll save 100 calories for every tablespoon you cut.

→ Substitute Splenda for sugar. If you're baking and need to keep the right proportion of dry ingredients, use Splenda Sugar Blend. It's part sugar and part Splenda, and you use the same amount you'd use of regular sugar. Here are some stats that will interest you in trying Splenda: Splenda has zero calories and zero carbs; regular granulated sugar has 17 calories per teaspoon and 775 calories per cup (with 200 grams of carbs per cup); Splenda Sugar Blend has half the calories and half the carbs of regular sugar.

→ Choose red sauce over white sauce. Creamy salad dressings are higher in calories than French, oil and vinegar, and vinaigrette. Tomato-based pasta sauce is lower in calories than a cream-based Alfredo sauce, 160 versus 50 calories for 2 ounces.

→ Use Egg Beaters instead of whole eggs. You'll save calories (more than half per serving: 1 egg is 75 calories, the Egg Beater equivalent is 30) and lower your chances of high cholesterol (Egg Beaters have no cholesterol; 1 egg has 210 mg—the American Heart Association says we should have less than 300 mg a day). You can also use egg whites instead of whole eggs in most recipes. The cholesterol and most of the calories are in the yolk.

When you reduce the calories in a recipe, it's not too hard to come up with a fairly accurate calorie count. Just add up the calories in each of the ingredients, then divide by the number of servings.

I'm sure the cooks in your family can make lots of other substitutions and reductions to create healthy, delicious recipes. You can help them by doing some online research and sharing what you learn.

For some great-tasting, healthy recipes, visit www.cuttingmyselfinhalf.com.

Index

About the Authors

Taylor LeBaron is an outgoing, articulate, and athletic seventeen-year-old who loves a challenge. He's a student technology leader for Chrysalis Experiential Academy in Roswell, GA. He and a small group of tech students repair computers and manage student entrepreneurial ventures. He is a student ambassador for his school and a member of the National Society of High School Scholars. He was chosen to carry the torch for the 2010 Winter Olympics.

Taylor started his own web-design business at thirteen, and he now repairs computers for families in his neighborhood. He enjoys electronics, history, travel, target practice, and working out. His college plans include a degree in business and economics.

When Taylor was fourteen, he took on his biggest challenge yet. He lost 150 pounds, literally cutting his body weight in half. He now views fitness as a lifestyle—one that changed, and added years to, his life.

Taylor and his family live in Ball Ground, GA. Visit Taylor at www.cuttingmyselfinhalf.com.

 **Jack and Mary Branson** have been writing as a team for six years and are working on their third and fourth books. Mary is the author of sixteen additional books. She has served as editing director and marketing director for national agencies.

Jack is a retired special agent with the U.S. Department of the Treasury, spending most of his career working in public corruption. His Secret Service duties included serving on the Presidential Jump Team and NATO's fiftieth anniversary. He is a licensed private investigator.

Jack holds a bachelor of science degree in business administration from Murray State University, Murray, Kentucky, where he also did graduate work. Mary holds a bachelor of arts degree in communication from Indiana University and did graduate work at Georgia State University.

The Bransons live in Cumming, GA. Visit them at www.jack andmarybranson.com.

A NOTE TO READERS

Taylor knows that his family history, coupled with his obesity, once made type 2 diabetes an almost certainty. Therefore, he plans to donate a portion of the proceeds from this book to Dr. Michael Dansinger's Diabetes Reversal Program at Tufts Medical Center. The program's mission is to coach patients and train medical professionals in the dietary and exercise methods known to achieve remission of type 2 diabetes. To find out more about this program, visit Dr. Dansinger's blog on WebMD (http://blogs.webmd.com/ life-with-diabetes-2).